Believe

Healthy Cooking in a Pinch

_The Family Cookbook on How to Create
Delicious Meals on Busy Days_

Enjoy!

Sheila Garcia

_XO_

Sheila Royce Garcia

For information, Sheila Royce Garcia at www.HealthyCookinginaPinch.com

Printed in the United States of America

ISBN: 0692247203
ISBN-13: 9780692247204

Food photos by 21Smiles Photography, http://www.facebook.com/21SmilesPhotography
Book cover design by Paper on Pine, www.paperonpine.com
Photos of Author by JNL Fitness Model Factory

I dedicate this book to all the amazing families, friends, and clients who have inspired me to share my secrets on cooking healthy meals in a pinch. I use to struggle with creating home-cooked meals due to my demanding to-do list. When I learned the secrets to creating a more balanced schedule, I returned to the kitchen to create healthy meals. Since then, I have become a more fit and fabulous mom.

It is my hope to inspire you to get back into the kitchen so that you and your family can live a healthier lifestyle.

In health and happiness,

Sheila

DISCLAIMER

The content provided in this book is designed to provide helpful information on the subjects discussed. The recommendations provided in this book are based on the author's own personal experience. Each person's physical, emotional, financial, and spiritual condition is unique. The publisher and author are not responsible for any specific health or allergy needs that may require medical supervision. The instruction in this book is not intended to replace or interrupt the reader's relationship with a physician or other professional. Please consult your doctor for matters pertaining to your specific health and diet. References are provided for informational purposes only and do not constitute endorsement of any websites or other sources. Readers should be aware that the websites listed in this book might change.

To contact the author, visit www.HealthyCookinginaPinch.com

CONTENTS

ACKNOWLEDGEMENTS

I wish to thank the following people for their support, contribution, encouragement and feedback in completing my first published cookbook.

To The Institute for Integrative Nutrition for their expertise, guidance, and positive feedback and for pushing me to complete my book.

To my parents, who gave their support and love. To my mom for teaching me her time-saving techniques for prepping meals on the weekend. She has continued to dedicate her time to doing so for many years.

To Linda, from 21Smiles Photography, for her timeless effort and who created beautiful food photography. To her daughter for testing my recipes and loving every bite.

To JNL Fitness Model Factory, for capturing my author and back cover photo from a beautiful location in the Hampton's. I am honored and blessed to work with Jennifer, Marli and Alex, you are a wonderful team.

To Lynne, who was inspired to learn the basic techniques for prepping meals so she could carry it over into her home and for enjoying my recipes.

To Heather, who was supportive and gave her positive feedback for my introduction and book title—and also, for sharing her delicious soup recipe for everyone to enjoy.

To Cindy, from Paper on Pine and her design team for their creative vision for designing a beautiful front and back book cover.

To all my family and friends who gave me feedback on my many book titles.

To my son, Nathan, who inspires me every day to believe that anything is possible.

INTRODUCTION

Welcome! This book was created for *you,* the busy family trying to juggle it all while short on time. Let's face it: when you are pressed for time, cooking healthy meals can be a challenge. With busy work schedules, activities, errands, and family obligations, it's no wonder we always find ourselves pinched for time to cook a family meal. My two secret ingredients for eating healthy are planning and preparation. These will guarantee that your family gets wholesome nutrition. As a holistic health coach, I hear many clients say, "I simply don't have the time to prepare a healthy meal after a long day." This leads them to a fast food venue or some other speedy option, spending more money than they should be and getting no nutritional value for their dollars.

Why empty your wallet on empty calories? Invest in your health, and let's make those positive shifts today to give your family the gift of energy, vitality, and glow. You will learn to make healthy, delicious meals that will stretch your money and save time in a pinch. In this cookbook, you will be inspired to make nutritious, delectable meals with a few of these time-saving tips:

- Use a slow cooker to help get dinner on the table effortlessly.
- Give leftovers a second life as a different meal.
- Cook once; eat two or three times.
- Make your meals for the week ahead of time using other preparation techniques.

Making your meals ahead of time could be your secret to a stress-free and successful week. Find the option that best fits your lifestyle.

You will also learn how to have a functional and inviting kitchen to cook in, eat healthy on any budget, pick fresh produce, eat healthy while on the run, and make delicious on-the-go snacks, as well as more than seventy healthy recipes.

As a busy mom, I needed to find a way to make healthy meals that were convenient for busy days. We all have those moments where we look in the freezer and see the meat we forgot to thaw, or peek in the refrigerator to see the veggies we forgot to cut, and decide that cooking isn't worth the trouble. I didn't want to fall into the rut of going out for fast, convenient foods, so I learned how to prep in a pinch. I decided to take a leaf from my mother's book. When I was growing up, she prepared meals for the week every Sunday. I took that knowledge to build a menu plan for my own home. Being prepared in advance is one of the best ways to keep you from running out to grab something "easy," because you already have a ready-to-prepare dinner at your fingertips.

What is *Healthy Cooking in a Pinch*? This cookbook is geared toward helping you design a menu based on your family's lifestyle. Pick a style that works for you. You may like to spend two days a week prepping your meals as opposed to just one day. Perhaps using the Crock-Pot is more convenient than making batches of food. The idea behind *Healthy Cooking in a Pinch* is to help you and your family feel more energetic and healthy in no time by preparing quality meals.

Some of the recipes listed were handed down by family that I have substituted with different ingredients, or recipes I have created throughout the years. These recipes are delicious and perfect for busy families like yours and mine.

Eating and cooking healthy meals for your family can be simple, so let's dive right in and get your culinary juices flowing.

Healthy Cooking
in a Pinch

CHAPTER 1:
Kitchen Transformation

When I was growing up, sitting down to eat five o'clock week-night dinners as a family was the norm. My father would come home from work to a healthy meal that was lovingly prepared by my mother. We all sat at the table with beautiful place settings and reflected on our day's events, told stories, and laughed while enjoying our food.

After I gave birth to my son, I struggled to create the same tradition for my own family. I was thrilled to be a mom, but I often relied on quick, convenient foods and checked my e-mails while eating to save time. I knew I needed to make changes in order to create a delicious lifestyle.

I'm sure you can relate to my story. These days, eating out and on the run is standard for many families. We've lost the magic of the home kitchen, which is the heart and hub of any home. As a busy mother, I found that the best way to live a healthy lifestyle was to adopt the same traditions I grew up with for my family. The first step in this process was to transform my kitchen to get my family and me healthy.

There are many health benefits in gathering together for family dinners in your home. Children tend to engage in positive behaviors and make healthier, more nutritious food choices. They can also help out in the kitchen, which can enhance their math skills as they learn how to read recipes, follow directions, and measure ingredients. Dinnertime at home bonds families together, which provides a sense of warmth and love. It is healthy for the mind, body, and soul.

Cooking allows you to get creative in the kitchen. – Sheila

When I began my personal journey to making home-cooked meals, I started slowly. I know you're busy, and cooking takes time, but the benefits are worth it. One of the best ways to start your journey is with an easy kitchen makeover. This is an inexpensive component of your planning and prepping. Here are a few tips to get you going in your healthy kitchen:

- *Declutter.* Get rid of the gadgets you don't use and put appliances and entertainment glassware that you only use once a year in storage. Make room on your shelves if you need it, or get a small shelving unit to help you stay organized. If you have a drawer filled with bills, place them in a file folder. What about your children's beautiful art work? Place it in a tote or wicker basket.
- *Get clear.* Clearing a space to cook can be more exhausting than actually preparing your meal, so make sure your pots and pans are organized and ready to go. Clean dishes on a regular basis—create a cleaning schedule if that helps.
- *Rehab your pantry.* Throw out processed snacks so you'll have more room for healthy choices. Check out my recommended staples for your pantry in chapter three for more ideas. This may be a challenge at first, however, by taking baby steps eventually it will become a part of your family's staple.
- *Boost the ambiance.* Get some fresh flowers or diffuse pure essential oils to make your kitchen more inviting. Fill the windowsill or baker's rack with a green plant or a pot of rosemary. Replace the cookie jar and cereal boxes with a bowl of fresh fruit or whole-foods energy bars that you can place in a decorative basket. Another great way to get a new feel in your kitchen is to paint your walls. If you have appliances on top of the counter, store them where they are out of the way but easily retrievable. Replace this space with a bottle of olive oil and vinegar.

Having an uncluttered countertop creates an environment in which you want to cook. Use these simple steps to be better acquainted with your kitchen and know that all the effort you put into it creates more love and health in your home. What could be better than enjoying good food, communication, and laughter together? When I know what ingredients are going into the food, I feel happier and know that I'm living a good life, and so is my family.

CHAPTER 2:
Planning Ahead

Eating healthy can be stress free and easy if you plan properly. Having a plan in place will create a successful road map toward your health. In this section, I will lay out some tips to get you on board with menu planning for those busy days. Taking this approach will save time, money, and stress, and, most importantly, it will contribute to your family's health. Here are a few simple tips:

Tip#1: Plan Your Meals

- Pick a day to sit down and plan your meals. Begin with picking a few ingredients to use a couple of times. For example: 1) penne pasta with cherry tomatoes 2) chicken and cherry tomato skewers 3) cucumber and cherry tomato salad. This will help you focus on what foods to buy and the ingredients you need before you embark on a grocery store adventure.
- Think of the foods that you and your family enjoy for breakfasts, lunches, dinners, and snacks. Once you put a list together, it will be easier to design a menu. Use the recipes in this cookbook to guide you in creating a healthy family menu.
- Create themes with your kids to make it fun. For example: no-meat Mondays, tasty Tuesdays, Crock-Pot Wednesdays, pasta Thursdays, etc. This can also help you get creative with dinner planning.
- If you work long hours, invest in a cooler to pack your meals for the day.

Tip #2: Make a Shopping List

- Write out your shopping list based on your menu.
- Take inventory of what you already have so you don't buy duplicates.
- Look for coupons and scan the grocery store circulars for the best prices.
- Take your delicious list and coupons, and go shopping.

- Buy in bulk if you have a family of healthy eaters for another option to savings. You can skip over to a warehouse in your area for bulk items.
- Eat a nutritious snack before your trip to the market to make sure you stick to your list. This way you are satisfied and full. You will become more mindful about sticking to the food items on your list.

Tip#3: Healthy Shopping

- Shop the perimeter of the grocery store. This is where you will find the whole foods. Avoid going in and out of the middle aisles and the temptation to throw in unwanted items that are not on your list.

Tip #4: Prep Your Meals

- Pick a day that allows you two or more hours to prep your meals.
- Gather your cutting board, utensils, BPA-free containers, Crock-Pot, mason jars, BPA-free freezer bags and BPA-free snack-sized bags.
- Gather your fruits and veggies to wash. I typically prepare big batches.
- Chop, slice, mince, and grate what you will need.
- Get your meats ready to marinade.
- Cook meals to freeze for a later date.
- Cook the food you would like to make in batches. For example: pancakes, breakfast muffins, meatballs, soups, or tomato sauce.

Tip #5: Helping Hands

- Recruit your kids and spouse to lend a hand in your delicious and healthy kitchen to make it a fun time together.
- Divide jobs so that one person washes the veggies while another chops, dices, and slices.

CHAPTER 3:
Healthy Staple Ideas and Prepping Tools

One of the key changes I made to improve my life significantly was to incorporate more whole foods. When I started this transformation, my energy levels lifted immediately, and I felt happy and healthy both inside and out. Nowadays, at my dinner table, I always have more plant-based foods than meat or complex carbohydrates, and I will often say, "Pass more plants, please." I usually create my veggies around the animal protein instead of the other way around. But, before we get too far in, let's talk a bit about whole foods.

Whole foods are foods that are in their natural state and haven't been stripped of their nutrients by chemical processes. These foods contain all the nutrition that our bodies need to function effectively. Whole foods provide our bodies with phytochemicals, enzymes, vitamins, minerals, fiber, and plenty of healthy antioxidants. Oh my, now that sounds delicious!

A perfect example of a whole food would be a potato, ripe from the farm. Once it is sliced and fried and various preservatives are added to it, it is no longer in its natural form.

Processed foods have become the number one staple in most family's homes. Processed foods contain additives, artificial colors, flavors, and preservatives. Integrating more whole foods into your life is key to living a healthy lifestyle. When you purchase whole foods, if possible, stick with locally grown or organic fruits and vegetables and organic and grass-fed meat that is unprocessed and contains no additives. While it's OK to indulge occasionally, like choosing a glass of red wine over green juice or a cookie over an apple, the important thing is to get as much of the recommended daily allowance of fruits and vegetables.

Tip: If you can't get organic greens, fruits, or vegetables, try soaking conventional produce in warm vinegar water. I usually use a teaspoon of apple cider vinegar to remove as much of the pesticides as possible.

Food Staples

This is a list of staples that I like to keep in my kitchen. It's not a shopping list to reflect the recipes in this cookbook, but you will find many ingredients listed that are used in this cookbook.

COMPLEX CARBOHYDRATES
Brown rice
Quinoa
Sweet potato
Whole grain pasta
Whole-wheat flour
Raw oatmeal (not instant)
Steel-cut oats
Granola
Whole grain bread
Beans: garbanzo, lentils, lima, cannellini, black beans, etc.

PROTEIN
Chicken or turkey (grilled or baked)
Lean fish (grilled or baked)
Salmon (wild caught is best), grilled, baked, or steamed
Lean pork tenderloin
Lean grass-fed red meat
Eggs
Greek yogurt
Plain yogurt

FRUITS
Berries
Cherries
Bananas

Apples
Melons
Mango
Pineapple
Pears
Kiwi
Limes
Lemons
Grapes

VEGGIES

Collard greens
Kale
Onions
Carrots
Cucumbers
Asparagus
Celery
Bell peppers
Broccoli
Cauliflower
Green beans
Tomatoes
Spinach
Lettuce
Squash

HEALTHY FATS

Virgin and Extra-virgin Olive oil
Avocados
Organic Coconut oil (unrefined)
Nuts (unsalted): walnuts, pecans, almonds
Seeds: pumpkin seeds, sunflower seeds
Peanut butter (try organic)

Almond butter
Sunflower butter
Fish oil
Sesame oil
Hummus

BEVERAGES
Water
Green tea
Herbal tea
Almond milk
Grass-fed milk

CONDIMENTS
Fresh and dried herbs and spices such as, cinnamon, nutmeg, basil, rosemary, chili powder, allspice, oregano, black pepper, etc.
Mustard
Dry white wine
Balsamic vinegar
Raw coconut aminos (soy-free seasoning sauce)
Sea salt
Pure vanilla extract
Pure maple syrup
Honey
Baking powder (aluminum free)
Baking soda

SEEDS
Hemp seeds (complete source of protein)
Flaxseeds (good source of omega-3 fatty acids)
Chia seeds (good source of omega-3 fatty acids and fiber)

Tools for Prepping

Every chef needs tools for prepping food in the kitchen.

Steamer basket

Grater

Peeler

Slow cooker

Mason jars—all sizes

Cutting board

Mixing bowls

Measuring cups and spoons

Chef's knife

Cooking utensils

Optional:

Juicer

Blender

Food processor

CHAPTER 4:
Meal-Prepping Styles

Let's face it; sometimes we don't have the time to spend hours in the kitchen each day. I will provide a few different prepping styles to help you prepare meals on busy days. Below you can explore a couple of my strategies for keeping your family satisfied on days when you're swamped. Pick a style that works for you.

Style #1—All in One Pot: The Slow Cooker

Slow cookers provide a wide variety of benefits. They cook with a low level of heat, which means that you can safely leave them unattended and expect tender meat when the cooking is complete. Many slow cooker recipes require less than twenty minutes of preparation. All you have to do is toss a few things in, set the timer, and serve hearty and healthy soups, stews, and casseroles when you return home.

Style #2—Cook Once: Eat Two, Three, or More Times

This is my favorite strategy for cooking for my family on busy days when I simply don't have enough time, but the process starts a few days before. On the days when I do have time to cook, usually on the weekends, I spend a few extra hours in the kitchen making portions far larger than my family could eat in a single meal. After dinner, I simply put the leftovers in containers, and freeze them for another night.

Some of my family's favorites are succulent soups and vegetable lasagnas. All you need to make the meals shine is a fresh element, and, luckily, this doesn't take much time at all. When I serve soup, I make a short stop at the supermarket and buy a loaf of fresh whole grain bread to serve with the soup. For the lasagna, I quickly whip up a salad to pair with it, and dinner is ready. Both meals take only a few minutes to prepare and always leave my family wanting more.

An even simpler strategy that I use is to cook enough for leftovers that we can eat again and again. My favorites are quinoa and brown rice, both of which are healthy and easy to prepare. I cook these grains in filtered water and leave them plain so I can add in different vegetables. You can eat some the next day for breakfast with fruit and nuts, or add it to a wrap or soup for lunch.

Once this is finished, I start the same process on another less busy day, and cook a whole chicken or turkey. We eat this for dinner that evening served with a sweet potato and side of in-season vegetables. The leftover poultry will find a second life the next day in either a sandwich or soup for lunch or tossed in a salad or whole-grain penne pasta for dinner.

Healthy cooking never tasted so good. – Sheila

Style #3—Ready, Set, Go!

Have you ever wished you could just push a button and, voilà, dinner would be served? It's a dream of every parent who comes home from a hard day at work and every stay-at-home mom who is busy taking care of her children all day. The reality is that we don't have a magic wand that can "Bibbidi-Bobbidi-Boo" a nutritious meal together. However, we can prepare to be ready and have the ingredients set so they can go in the oven as soon as we walk through the door. Here are my time-saving hot tips.

On a less busy day, prepare a pork tenderloin, chicken or turkey roast, or chicken breasts with all the trimmings. Place the meat in a large zip-lock bag and marinade it in honey mustard or lemons with garlic, rosemary and olive oil. Put your favorite veggies and a few red potatoes in a separate plastic bag. You can keep them in the refrigerator for about two days. Take note of the expiration dates. Once you arrive home, preheat the oven, get your dinner out of the bags, place into a glass pan, and cook it in the oven. All you need to do is sit back, relax, and wait until dinner is done!

Tip: If you buy these items in bulk, you can even make a few freezer meals. Store all three components in separate freezer bags. Make sure you write the date on the bags.

Another time-saving tip is to wash and cut up all your favorite vegetables for the week. On a less busy day, gather your vegetables. I like yellow squash, bell peppers, broccoli, onions, asparagus, green beans, cauliflower, mushrooms, or whatever is in season. I dice or slice my favorite veggies to be ready for my salads, sauté, steam basket, or stir-fry. All the preparation has been done so all you need to do is throw your favorite vegetables in the pan, oven, or steam basket for dinner. This is great for veggie pizza night because all the work is done for you. You can do the same with your fruit.

Tip: If you cut your fruits in advance, you can squeeze the juice of a lemon or orange on them to keep them from turning brown.

Style #4—Stock Up Your Freezer Party
Getting a few friends together to prep freezer meals is a good style when you're in a pinch. You can host the party and invite a couple of friends over to help make the meals. Have each pick one or two recipes so that everyone can walk home with a few meals.

This is a great way to engage with your friends, have fun, and taste test each recipe. Don't forget the music.

CHAPTER 5:
Eating Healthy on Any Budget

Millions of people believe that eating healthy isn't possible on a budget. The truth is that you can eat healthy on any budget. By following the tips below, you can enjoy healthy food...even if you have limited resources.

Know which Produce to Buy

Eating fruits and vegetables is important. However, if purchasing everything "organic" doesn't fit your budget, then it's a good idea to buy only "organic" produce that's on the "Dirty Dozen" list. This list is found on the Environmental Working Group website. Please visit www.ewg.org for updates.

PRODUCE TO PURCHASE ORGANIC

This is a short list of produce with high concentrations of pesticides according to the information provided on the Environmental Working Group website.

Here are some examples of produce I purchase "organic" based on the information I read on the above website:

- Apples
- Celery
- Cherry Tomatoes
- Spinach
- Strawberries

In addition, you'll want to purchase organic kale, collard greens, and summer squash.

PRODUCE TO PURCHASE NONORGANIC

This is a short list of produce found on the Environmental Working Group website considered safe and with low concentrations of pesticides. Therefore, you don't need to spend money on organic fruits and veggies.

Included are:

1. Asparagus
2. Avocado
3. Eggplant
4. Kiwi
5. Pineapples

Organic versus Nonorganic: What's Cheaper and Healthier?

Nonorganic products are usually cheaper than organic. Therefore, if you'd like to eat organic foods here are four tips to help you do so on a budget:

- Buy nonorganic produce considered safe and with low concentrations of pesticides. If you're on a budget, then attempting to eat everything organic can be expensive. Instead, save money by *only* buying organic produce that is on the "Dirty Dozen" list provided by the Environmental Working Group website.
- Save money by buying store-brand organic foods. Many grocery stores, including discount chain markets, have developed their own line of organic foods. This is an excellent way to eat organic at a lower price.
- Get organic coupons. Many organic brands offer coupons if you register on their websites or follow them on social media platforms.
- Start your own garden. Even if you live in an apartment, you can grow some items on your balcony, patio, or windowsill. If you're unable to garden on your own, then seek out local food co-ops.

More Ways to Eat Healthy on Any Budget— Organic and Nonorganic

Buy Locally and In-Season

If you're looking to lower your costs while enjoying fresher produce, then buy local...and in-season. Local produce is often more affordable because you're buying it directly from the farmers. This cuts out most, if not all, of the "middlemen."

Save with Bulk

You can save money by buying healthier foods in bulk. In addition, don't limit buying in bulk to your local grocery store. While at farmers' markets, ask if they'll give you a discount for purchasing larger amounts.

Following are foods to consider buying in bulk:

- Fish, poultry, and meat
- Potatoes
- Frozen veggies
- Whole-grain products
- Dried beans
- Dried peas
- Nuts (raw or dry-roasted)

Always Plan

Every week, invest thirty to sixty minutes to preparing your shopping list. Your preplanned shopping list is the best way to avoid impulse purchases. It only takes two or three impulse purchases each week to destroy your budget. Furthermore, never do your grocery shopping when you're hungry. You're far more likely to make impulse purchases when you're hungry. (Refer to chapter 2.)

Try Coupons

Coupons are an excellent way to eat healthy on a budget, whether you're buying organic or nonorganic. There's no need for you to devote hours of your time searching for coupons. There are blogs and websites that can help you with that.

Important: Many people use coupons to save money on foods that are highly processed and unhealthy. Remember, your goal is to eat healthy on a budget, not eat junk more affordably. Soda, chips, and cookies provide you little nutrition while inflating your weekly grocery bill.

Follow Your Money

You might be surprised what you discover when you follow your money.

- How frequently do you eat out?
- How much money do you spend daily for snacks, coffee, and/or lunch?

Evaluating and paying attention to the amount of money you spend on junk or unhealthy foods is an excellent way to both save money and also cut down on, or stop eating, unhealthy foods such as:

- Soda
- Cookies
- Crackers
- Processed foods
- Prepackaged meals

Eating healthy on a budget is much easier after you've followed your money. Both your body and pocketbook will be better off.

Love What's Left

Some people will follow all the above tips. They'll save money and eat healthy...yet refuse to eat leftovers.

Do you hate leftovers or refuse to eat them? Consider that every time you throw your leftovers in the garbage, you're actually tossing your hard-earned money in the trash.

For those who hate leftovers, here are two suggestions:

- Get creative. Try using your leftovers in new ways or spice them up.
- Reduce the amount of food you cook. Make smaller servings. Prepare only enough food for you or your family. (Refer to chapter 4.)

It's Possible

It is indeed possible for you to eat healthy on a budget. You don't have to go broke.

Following the practical tips and suggestions above, you can eat well without spending an excessive amount of time...or money. You'll save money, eat healthier, and be happy.

CHAPTER 6:
Guide to Picking Fresh Produce

Have you ever wondered how long it took "Mr. Broccoli" to travel before it reached your fork?

The average meal travels thousands of miles before reaching your plate. You can think about it in terms of your weekly, monthly, and yearly consumption, but it boils down to the fact that food travels much farther than it should to reach the average family plate each day.

As a holistic health coach, I always instruct my clients to make conscious decisions when it comes to selecting how and where to purchase their food. Moreover, I suggest that they select local agriculture or start their own gardens. While it may seem easier to grab your fruits and vegetables from the market, there are several advantages that make home gardening or buying local produce far more rewarding.

#1 Freshness
- There truly is nothing like biting into a fresh, crisp fruit or vegetable, which is why the first advantage to buying local produce is unmatched freshness. When you purchase your fruits and vegetables from a local farmers' market or pick them from your own backyard, you get food that is fresh off the tree, plant, or vine, guaranteeing the best possible taste.

#2 Saving Money
- While it can be expensive to buy local produce, there are ways to do it and save money in the end. One of the most cost-effective and least known methods is Community Supported Agriculture (CSA). This process involves buying a *share* from a farmer before the growing season begins. In return, you receive fresh produce later in the season. The farmer gets access to cash flow before the season, and you get fresh fruit at a reduced cost. It's win-win.

- Although it can be time consuming, starting your own garden can save you money. Also, there is nothing like going out to your backyard when you want a fresh cucumber and tomato for your salad.

#3 Supporting the Community

- Buying locally develops and supports the community. While the financial benefit to local farmers and producers is more obvious, you also get a chance to build a better bond with your family, friends, neighbors, and overall community. You can meet plenty of new people while visiting farmers' markets, and Community Supported Agriculture programs give you a chance to meet local farmers and learn about where your food really comes from.

So, next time you're deciding where to purchase your produce, I encourage you to buy locally or start your own garden. You'll save money, enjoy the taste of fresh foods, and build bonds that can last a lifetime.

To find a CSA (Community Supported Agriculture) in your area please visit www.localharvest.org.

CHAPTER 7:
Healthy Eating for Travel and Parties

Many of us struggle with eating healthy during special occasions and trips. The biggest challenges most people face are:

- Not preparing what to eat during vacations or at parties.
- Picking wrong food choices when you are constantly on the run.
- Fatigue and stress from celebrations and travel that can lead to emotional eating.

Here are a few tips to help you eat healthier.

How to Eat Healthy for Special Occasions

- Stick with a healthy snack.
- Drink plenty of water throughout the day to keep yourself hydrated and feeling fuller.
- Make mindful choices when filling your plate with food. Put vegetables on your plate first and then see how much room is left for meat and a carbohydrate.
- Try to stick to your regular healthy regimen during the event, holiday, or vacation. If you overindulge during the celebration, get back to your healthy way of eating the next day.
- Practice mindful eating. So what is mindful eating? A) Take time to notice what is on your plate—the color, smell, flavor, and texture. B) Put your fork down after each bite. C) Chew your food and eat slowly. D) Avoid distractions.

Tips on Prepping Your Meals for Vacation

Follow the same tips I laid out for you in chapter 4. This will be easy if you get a condo, rental house, or hotel room with an eat-in style kitchen. If you travel by car, prepare your meals in advance and place them in a cooler. If you are flying, I recommend taking an extra day to go grocery shopping where you vacation and reserve a couple hours to prep your meals.

Here are a few tips on eating healthy if you don't have a kitchen:

- Prepare your own grab-and-go snacks that you can take in the car, swimming pool, or beach. Refer to chapter 9. These choices will curb your appetite and help you from reaching for unhealthy snacks
- Instead of eating out every night, take a trip to the grocery store or farmers' market. At the farmers' market, you are surrounded by every color of the rainbow and whole, nutritious foods. At the grocery store, you can find healthy hot foods already prepared for you to take back to your hotel room for dinner. As an added bonus, you will have more money in your pocketbook.

How to Avoid Event Dessert Temptations

- Have a sweet vegetable such as carrots, sweet potato, or squash (spaghetti squash) with your dinner.
- Try eating a protein like nuts or lean meat first, and then see if you are still hungry for that sweet.
- Drink a glass of water, and then see if you want that piece of cake.
- Bring a healthy fruit platter or bowl of trail mix to the event.
- Avoid mindless munching by eating a healthy snack before you go to your event, or step aside from the dessert table and mingle with the talkers, not the eaters.

If you would like to learn about my coaching services, please visit www.SheilaFitnessNHealthyLifestyle.com

CHAPTER 8:
7-Day Sample Menu for the Everyday Family

A. Create a week or two of menus. I created a sample for you here.

B. Create a shopping list.

C. Go Shopping.

D. Pick a prep day and style that works for you. Refer to chapter 4.

What is home cooking? Delicious meals made with love. — Sheila

Day 1
Breakfast: Oatmeal Pumpkin Pancakes   61
Lunch: Jicama Salsa on top of mixed greens   84
Dinner: Veggie Burger with a side of Jicama Salsa   78, 84
Snacks: Trail Mix and On-the-Go Veggies.   41, 40

Day 2
Breakfast: Busy Bee Smoothie   72
Lunch: Veggie Wrap   81
Dinner: Whole Chicken in a slow cooker, with Roasted Orange
Asparagus and side of brown rice   107, 108
Snacks: Smoothie and Trail Mix   42, 41

Day 3
Breakfast: Summertime Oatmeal   57
Lunch: Cranberry Chicken Salad (using leftover chicken from day 2)   92
Dinner: Salmon with Tomatoes and Veggies   122
Snacks: Heavenly Hard-Boiled Egg   46

Day 4
Breakfast: Chocolate Surprise   71
Lunch: Savory Turkey Wimpies in a Bowl   89
Dinner: Raw Rainbow Salad with Halibut   120, 127
Snacks: Cinnamon Popcorn and Trail Mix   43, 41

Day 5

Breakfast: Raw Cereal	59
Lunch: Leftover Savory Turkey Wimpies from day 4 on a whole grain roll	89
Dinner: Fish Tacos using leftover halibut from day 4 served with salsa, chopped green onions, black beans, and chopped cilantro on hard-shelled tacos with Guacamole Dip	44
Snacks: Berry-Nut Yogurt and Trail Mix	47, 41

Day 6

Breakfast: Berry Delicious Pancakes	63
Lunch: Apple and Pecan Salad	90
Dinner: Lazy Stuffed Pepper Soup	125
Snacks: On-the-Go Veggies and Kale Chips	40, 39

Day 7

Breakfast: Fiesta Egg Burrito	67
Lunch: Leftover Lazy Stuffed Pepper Soup (from day 6)	125
Dinner: Scallops Marinara with Whole Grain Pasta	124
Snacks: Organic Apple Chips and Glorious Rice Cake	39, 46

CHAPTER 9:
No-Fuss Healthy Snacks

H ere are some of my favorite and simple healthy snacks.

Organic Kale Chips

1 bunch organic kale
½ to 1 tablespoon olive oil
A pinch of sea salt or Mrs. Dash seasoning

Preheat oven to 350°F.

Wash and dry the kale and remove stems. Cut leaves into pieces. Spray olive oil on a baking sheet. Spread leaves evenly on the sheet and massage olive oil through.

Bake about 15 to 20 minutes, until the edges of the leaves turn slightly brown. The kale should be crisp before removing. Add either sea salt or Mrs. Dash seasoning.

Organic Apple Chips

This is a great afternoon snack and delicious served with hummus.

4 medium red apples, thinly sliced
1 to 2 tablespoons unrefined organic coconut oil, melted
1 to 2 teaspoons cinnamon
¼ teaspoon sea salt

Preheat oven to 300°F. Wash and core apples. Next, thinly cut apples by hand or use a food processor. Lightly coat a large baking sheet with coconut oil. Sprinkle cinnamon and sea salt and mix. Bake for 1 hour and 15 minutes until crisp, turning once halfway through. Allow to cool before serving.

On-the-Go Veggies

Organic celery
Jicama (this is a root vegetable that looks similar to a turnip)
Organic cucumbers
Yellow squash
Organic bell peppers (kids like the sweeter ones)
Carrots
Cauliflower
Sugar snap peas
Skinny asparagus
Seasonings: sea salt, black pepper, Mrs. Dash seasoning, or garlic
and ginger powders
Lemon juice (optional)
Olive oil or grape seed oil (optional)

Cut the veggies into sticks or cubes. Sprinkle with seasoning. You
can also squeeze lemon juice and a drizzle of olive oil or grape seed
oil into a bag, add veggies, and massage or shake.

Option: Spread almond or sunflower butter on a red bell pepper
(kids usually love this).

Take-to-Work Trail Mix

1 cup almonds
½ cup sunflower seeds
½ cup chopped pecans
½ cup unsweetened dried cranberries
½ cup unsweetened raisins
½ cup goji berries
¼ cacao nibs
Organic shredded coconut
½ teaspoon cinnamon
¼ teaspoon nutmeg
1 to 2 tablespoons chia seeds (optional)
Grape seed oil, macadamia nut oil, or coconut oil.

Mix a handful of each of the above ingredients in a bowl, and store in a mason jar, snack bags, or containers. You can either roast the nuts or keep them raw.

Option: For a spicy version, roast the nuts with chili pepper or cayenne pepper and dried cilantro. Place the nuts on a baking sheet, add seasoning, and drizzle with oil. Roast the nuts at 350°F degrees for about 5 minutes or until slightly brown.

Smoothies

Refer to chapter 14 for recipes

You can prepare all the ingredients the night before and place in your blender so that all you have to do is hit the blend button the next day for your breakfast or midmorning or afternoon snack.

Sweet Roasted Chickpeas

1-15 ounce can of garbanzo beans
1 to 2 tablespoons olive oil
½ teaspoon cinnamon
¼ teaspoon sea salt
2 to 3 tablespoons pure maple syrup

Preheat oven to 425°F. Place the chickpeas on a paper towel and pat dry. You can leave the skin on, or peel it off.

Lightly coat a baking sheet with olive oil and place your chick peas evenly across. Drizzle with a little more olive oil and sprinkle with cinnamon and sea salt. Drizzle maple syrup over and massage through. Bake in the oven for 15 minutes, then toss and bake for another 10 to 15 minutes until golden brown.

On-the-Go Popcorn

¼ cup unrefined organic coconut oil, melted (for the pot)
½ cup organic popcorn kernels
¼ cup cranberries or raisins
¼ cup pecans
1 tablespoon organic butter (to drizzle on top of the popcorn)
¼ teaspoon sea salt
1 tablespoon cinnamon

In a medium pot, add coconut oil and popcorn kernels. Cover pot with the lid slightly ajar and cook on medium heat. Keep an eye on the popcorn. Once popped, pour popcorn into a large bowl. Drizzle with melted organic butter. Next, mix in cranberries or raisins, pecans, sea salt, and cinnamon.

Guacamole Dip

Not only is this a great dip, but you can also spread it on a chicken wrap, spoon a dollop on your grilled burger, add it to your tacos, or layer it on top of your tortilla. Guacamole dip is healthy, versatile, and delicious.

2 ripened avocados
1 tablespoon freshly squeezed lemon juice
1 tablespoon red onion, minced
1 garlic clove, minced
1 teaspoon chili powder
1½ tablespoons jalapeño chili pepper, minced
½ tablespoon olive oil
½ tablespoon low sodium Worcestershire sauce
½ tablespoon balsamic vinegar
1 teaspoon cumin powder
½ teaspoon sea salt
1 to 2 tablespoons fresh organic cilantro, finely chopped

Peel the avocados and remove the pits. Add the avocados to a bowl and mash with the lemon juice. Add the red onion, garlic, and chili powder, and mix well. Add the jalapeño chili pepper, olive oil, Worcestershire sauce, balsamic vinegar, cumin, salt, and cilantro.

Mix well. Refrigerate for 45 minutes to 1 hour before serving. You can serve this in a bowl or in individual cups to dip your veggies, or spread on flax seed crackers.

Yield: 1 cup

Glorious Rice Cake

This isn't so much a recipe as a great snack option for after school or when you are on-the-go.

Any flavor rice cake (plain has less sugar and calories)
Coconut, sunflower, or almond butter
Raw honey and cinnamon or nutmeg (optional)

Spread butter on rice cake. Drizzle with raw honey and cinnamon or nutmeg, if using.

Heavenly Hard-Boiled Egg

½ dozen organic eggs
3 tablespoons hummus
12 oil-packed sundried tomatoes, already cut
2 tablespoons pine nuts
¼ cup fresh cilantro or fresh basil, washed and chopped

In a medium pot of water, drop a few eggs in and bring to a boil. The eggs should be cooked in about 10 minutes. Take the eggs out and set aside to cool. Once cooled, peel the eggs and cut in half. Discard the yolk. For each half of the egg, scoop about ½ tablespoon of hummus, add 1 or 2 sundried tomatoes and a few pine nuts, and garnish with either cilantro or basil. It's heavenly delicious—great for a party.

Berry-Nut Yogurt

1 cup Greek yogurt, plain
¼ cup blueberries
1 tablespoon pecans
1 tablespoon cacao nibs
¼ teaspoon cinnamon

Scoop yogurt into a bowl or small mason jar. Add berries, pecans, cacao nibs, and cinnamon.

Avocado Snack

1 whole avocado
Pinch of sea salt
1 tablespoon olive oil

Wash and cut avocado in half. Take out the pit and discard. Cut the avocado into 1/3-inch slices. Add a pinch of sea salt and drizzle with olive oil.

CHAPTER 10:
Breakfast

A healthy breakfast is the best way to start your day off right. These delicious breakfast options provide both great taste and great nutrition.

Quinoa for Energy

I love to start my morning with a bowl of quinoa. This is a delicious superfood that provides both energy and satisfaction. It is packed with antioxidants and is a great source of protein.

Time-saving tip: You can place all the dry ingredients together in a bowl, mason jar, or plastic bag the night before.

1 cup filtered water
1 cup quinoa milk
Pinch sea salt
1 cup organic, whole-grain, sprouted quinoa
½ cup organic blueberries
Handful of sliced almonds
½ teaspoon cinnamon
1 tablespoon hemp seeds (optional)
½ tablespoon chia seeds (optional)

Bring water and milk to a boil, add a pinch of sea salt. Pour in quinoa. Cover and turn heat to low. Simmer 15 to 20 minutes or until fluffy. Mix in the blueberries, almonds, cinnamon, and hemp and chia seeds if you are using them. Drizzle extra milk over quinoa bowl if desired.

Serves 4

Quinoa Berry Muffins

This is a delicious breakfast for on-the-go or a tasty snack any time of day. These muffins will become an instant family favorite.

Time-saving tip: Make batches and freeze for busy days.

1 cup cooked quinoa
2½ cups raw oats
2 ripe bananas
1 teaspoon cinnamon
½ teaspoon celtic sea salt
1 teaspoon baking powder
1 cup berries (choose your favorite)
¼ cup pure maple syrup
2 tablespoons unrefined organic coconut oil, melted
1 teaspoon vanilla extract
1 egg

Preheat oven to 375°F. Cook quinoa according to instructions on the box. Mix dry ingredients in a medium bowl. In another bowl, mix wet ingredients. Next, combine dry and wet ingredients together. Mix until smooth. Fill a cupcake pan with 8 liners. Add ¼ cup of mix to each liner.

Bake 20 to 25 minutes

Serves 8

Oatmeal in a Slow Cooker

Oatmeal is nutritious and warms the body from the inside out. I love to give my slow cooker a good workout and enjoy a bowl of warm oatmeal in the morning. Throw everything in the night before, and the following morning, breakfast is served. I do this often because I know my family is getting a good nutritious breakfast.

Time-saving tip: If you have extra, you can add it to your midmorning or lunch smoothie.

1 tablespoon organic butter
1 ⅔ cups whole-grain rolled oats (make sure it states gluten free on the package)
2 cups filtered water
2 cups almond milk, unsweetened
Pinch sea salt
1 tablespoon ground flaxseed
1 tablespoon organic honey
1 cup organic apples, cut in cubes leaving skin on
Handful of walnuts

Coat the inside of the slow cooker with organic butter.
Pour oats, water, milk, and sea salt in the slow cooker, cover and cook on low for eight hours.

Following morning, add one cup of oatmeal to a bowl. Add flax seeds, honey, apples, or walnuts. Breakfast is served!

Optional: drizzle extra milk over oatmeal bowl.

Serves 4

Baked Apple Oatmeal Cake

This recipe makes a hectic morning a little simpler and sweeter. It's one of my favorites. This also makes a delicious dessert.

Time-saving tip: You can prepare this the night before, and place in the refrigerator until the next morning.

2½ cups gluten-free oats
½ teaspoon cinnamon
½ teaspoon nutmeg
¼ cup raisins
1 tablespoon chia seeds (optional)
1 teaspoon baking powder
½ teaspoon sea salt
2 cups almond milk, vanilla
1 cup peeled, diced apples
3 tablespoons pure maple syrup
For topping (optional):
2 tablespoons butter
1 tablespoon organic sugar
½ teaspoon cinnamon
½ cup pecans

The night before, lightly coat an eight-inch glass pan with butter and dust with flour. In a medium bowl, mix all the dry ingredients together. In a separate bowl, mix all the wet ingredients. Next, mix the dry and wet ingredients and place in the glass pan.

The next morning, preheat the oven to 375°F and place the glass pan in the oven for 30 to 45 minutes until golden brown.

Optional: For topping, melt the butter and mix in the sugar, cinnamon, and pecans. After 25 minutes, take the oatmeal out of the oven and spread with topping. Place back in the oven for another 15 to 20 minutes.

Serves 8 to 12

Summertime Oatmeal

This is another time-saving recipe for busy parents. What I love about it is that family members can make their favorite kind. Once prepared, all you do is open the refrigerator in the morning, and breakfast is ready.

Time-saving tip: You can make a bunch of oatmeal in a mason jar on a less busy day, and it will keep for two to three days in a sealed jar.

A couple mason jars
1 cup raw oats per mason jar
1 cup almond milk per jar
1 teaspoon cinnamon per jar
½ tablespoon pure maple syrup per jar
½ tablespoon chia seeds per jar
A few of your favorite summer berries: blueberries, strawberries, blackberries, or raspberries
1 tablespoon of your favorite nut, for topping
Optional: You can also have apples, pears, or peaches washed and ready to add.

In a small bowl, mix the raw oats with milk, cinnamon, pure maple syrup, chia seeds, fruit, and nut. Spoon into your mason jar and refrigerate overnight. You can keep each jar up to three days.

1 serving

Bahama Mama Steel-Cut Oats

This will get you dancing in the kitchen first thing in the morning. It reminds me of going to a tropical island.

Time-saving tip: Chop your fruit ahead of time and have dry ingredients ready to go in a small container or bag.

1½ cups coconut water or water
1½ cups coconut milk
Pinch of sea salt
1 cup organic steel-cut oats
½ banana, sliced
¼ cup chopped pineapple
1 tablespoon organic unsweetened shredded coconut
1 tablespoon chopped pecans

Bring coconut water and milk to a boil. Add sea salt and oats. Reduce heat to low, cover pot, and simmer for 15 to 20 minutes. When finished, add sliced bananas and chopped pineapple and simmer for a few more minutes. You can sprinkle with shredded coconut and pecans.

Serves 4

Raw Cereal

This is a heart-healthy cereal that will give your family energy to start the day. This recipe is fun because you can mix it up and add any kind of fruit or seeds. My son loves to help me prepare this for the week. This is one antioxidant powerhouse.

Time-saving tip: You can buy the dry ingredients in bulk and prepare extra. Store in an airtight container. Mason jars are my favorite.

½ tablespoon ground flaxseed
1 tablespoon sliced almonds
¼ cup raw oats
1 tablespoon wheat germ
Pinch of cinnamon
½ teaspoon chia seeds
1 tablespoon sunflower seeds
1 medium crisp Fuji apple
1 tablespoon blueberries
¼ sliced banana
½ cup of unsweetened almond, hemp, or quinoa milk

Add all dry ingredients and mix. Next, shred the apple and add more of your favorite fruit. In addition to the apple, I like to add blueberries and bananas to this recipe. Last, add your milk. (Tip: you can add dried fruit such as, raisins, cranberries or dates).

Serves 1

Oatmeal-Pumpkin Pancakes

Oatmeal-pumpkin pancakes are oh-so-good, especially during autumn when leaves are starting to fall and pumpkins are everywhere.

Time-saving tip: Make extra on a day when you're not so busy and store in the freezer (use parchment paper in between so they don't stick together) for during the week.

1 cup gluten-free oats (buy the one that states gluten free because some oats are manufactured in a facility with wheat)
½ cup pureed pumpkin
2 tablespoons almond milk, vanilla
1 egg
¼ teaspoon nutmeg
½ teaspoon cinnamon
2 tablespoons pure maple syrup
1 tablespoon hemp seeds (optional)
1 to 2 tablespoons unrefined coconut oil, melted (for the skillet)

In a blender, combine oats, pureed pumpkin, milk, egg, nutmeg, cinnamon, maple syrup and hemp seeds. Blend until smooth. Next, melt the coconut oil in a skillet on medium high heat. Drop about ¼ cup of batter onto skillet. Cook until edges are golden brown. Flip and cook for 1 to 2 minutes. Serve on a warm plate and drizzle with pure maple syrup.

Serves 4

Whole Grain Pumpkiny Pumpkin Pancakes

What better way to start your day than with a little pumpkin for breakfast? Did you know that this squash is not only versatile but comes with a wealth of healthy benefits? Pumpkins are low in calories and rich in the antioxidant beta-carotene as well as vitamins and fiber.

Time-saving tip: Make extra ahead of time and store in the freezer (use parchment paper between each pancake so they don't stick together) for during the week.

1 tablespoon ground flaxseeds (optional)
1 tablespoon chia seeds (optional)
1½ cups organic whole wheat flour
3 tablespoons organic sugar or ¾ teaspoon of powdered vanilla stevia
½ teaspoon baking soda
½ teaspoon baking powder
½ teaspoon nutmeg, cinnamon, and ginger
Dash sea salt
½ ripe banana, mashed
1½ cups pumpkin spice coconut milk (or vanilla almond milk)
½ teaspoon organic vanilla extract
1 tablespoon unrefined organic coconut oil, melted
Optional: ½ cup of pecans or sliced almonds

Preheat oven to 425°F

Mix all the dry ingredients together in a bowl. In a separate bowl, mix mashed banana with all the wet ingredients. Whisk the dry ingredients in with the wet.

Place parchment paper on baking sheet. Scoop ¼ cup pancake batter onto the baking sheet and sprinkle a couple of nuts on top. Bake for 20 minutes or until edges are slightly golden brown.

Berry Delicious Pancakes

These fruit-filled pancakes are a sweet hit. If you want additional protein, you can top with a dollop of plain Greek yogurt.

Time-saving tip: Make extra for those busy mom days during the week. You can heat them up in the oven or pop one or two in your toaster. This way you and your family will get in a healthy breakfast before your day starts.

1 ⅓ cups unsweetened almond or hemp milk
2 tablespoons freshly squeezed lemon juice
½ teaspoon lemon zest
2 teaspoons pure maple syrup
1¼ cups whole wheat flour
2 teaspoons stevia (powdered) or 4 tablespoons organic sugar
1 tablespoon baking powder
½ teaspoon baking soda
½ teaspoon cinnamon
1 tablespoon ground flaxseed (optional)
Blueberries and raspberries

In a medium bowl, mix milk, lemon juice, lemon zest, and pure maple syrup together. Add all dry ingredients and mix until batter is smooth. Let stand for 1 to 2 minutes.

Heat a medium-sized skillet or griddle over medium heat. Lightly coat with coconut oil or cooking spray. Fill ¼ cup with batter, pour onto griddle, and add berries. Cook until it bubbles and the edges are slightly golden brown. Flip to cook the other side.

Enjoy this healthy version of pancakes.

Serves 8

Protein Pancake Muffins to Go

These make a great breakfast to take with you on-the-go, while you travel, or just for fun. They include hemp seeds, which contain essential amino acids and are a good source of protein.

Time-saving tip: Make extra and store in a reclosable plastic bag in the freezer.

1 cup whole wheat flour (you can substitute gluten-free pancake mix)
1 tablespoon organic sugar
2 teaspoons aluminum-free baking powder
¼ teaspoon salt
1 tablespoon hemp seeds (optional)
1 teaspoon cinnamon
1 egg
1 cup hemp milk
2 tablespoons olive oil
3 tablespoons pure maple syrup
Optional: Add your favorite berries.

Preheat the oven to 350°F. Lightly coat muffin pans with coconut oil and a little flour or fill with cupcake liners.

In a medium bowl, mix dry ingredients and wet ingredients separately, then mix together. Fill each muffin cup halfway with pancake mix. Place in the oven for about 20 minutes until edges are slightly golden brown. Enjoy warm or cool. You can drizzle a little pure maple syrup or spread some organic jelly on top.

Serves 6 to 8

Sunny-Side Up Egg on a Whole Grain Muffin

Anything that says "sunny" will surely brighten your morning. This is a great protein and complex carbohydrate combo to keep your family smiling until lunch. I usually serve this with a side of fruit and freshly squeezed juice.

Time-saving tip: Wash the tomatoes, scallions, and cilantro ahead of time, so all you need to do in the morning is toast the English muffin and fry your egg.

1 whole egg
½ of a whole-grain English muffin (if you prefer a sandwich, use a whole English muffin)
1 tablespoon plain hummus
2 sliced plump tomatoes
½ tablespoon scallion, finely chopped
2 sprigs cilantro, finely chopped
1 teaspoon olive oil

Heat a small skillet and lightly coat with olive oil. Break the fresh egg onto the skillet and fry until bottom of egg browns lightly. Toast the English muffin in a toaster. On a cutting board, using a knife finely chop the scallion and cilantro. Remove the English muffin from the toaster and spread with hummus, layer with plump to-matoes (2 to 4 slices), add the fried egg, and top with scallions and chopped cilantro.

Serves 1

Fiesta Egg Burrito

This is a great way to spice up your morning and a great option for a busy day. This also works great for lunch or dinner.

Time-saving tip: Get everything but the eggs ready ahead of time.

1 whole egg
½ cup cheddar cheese
1 tablespoon olive oil
1 tablespoon fresh chopped cilantro
1 tablespoon red onion, finely chopped (optional)
2 slices avocado
1 whole grain tortilla
¼ cup salsa (optional)

In a medium bowl, whisk the egg and cheese. In a skillet, warm olive oil on low to medium heat. Add egg mixture; cook until no longer runny. Get a cutting board and finely chop cilantro and red onion. Next, cut an avocado in half and remove the pit. On a cutting board, scoop one half of the avocado out of the shell and slice. Store extra avocado slices in a container.

Turn the oven to 350°F and warm a tortilla for about 30 seconds. Take it out and place the egg mixture in the middle. Add cilantro, red onions, 2 avocado slices, and wrap. Serve with a side of salsa.

Serves 1

Kids' Veggie and Egg Pizza

Pizza for breakfast! What a fantastic idea. This is a fun way to get your kiddos to eat their eggs.

Time-saving tip: Prepare everything except the eggs ahead of time.

1 medium whole grain or gluten-free crust (round or square)
1 whole tomato, sliced
1 cup shredded pizza cheese
1 cup sliced mushrooms
3 or 4 eggs, depending on size of crust
¼ cup spinach leaves, shredded
Sea salt and pepper to taste

Preheat the oven to 425°F (look at the pizza crust package). Place the crust on a baking sheet or stone lightly coated with olive oil. Evenly place sliced tomatoes on the crust and sprinkle with cheese, and mushrooms. Crack 3 or 4 eggs evenly on the crust and toss spinach leaves on top. Sprinkle sea salt and pepper to taste. Place in the oven for 7 to 10 minutes until cheese is melted, the whites of the egg and yolk look golden, and the crust is golden brown around the edges. Serve warm.

Serves 2 to 4

Family Quesadillas for Breakfast

I hope you're hungry. These are perfect for a Saturday morning when you have time to enjoy with the family.

1 cup roasted cherry tomatoes
Sea salt and black pepper to taste
2 large eggs
1 garlic clove, minced
¼ cup shredded mozzarella cheese
½ cup sundried tomatoes
½ cup basil
2 whole-wheat tortillas
1 to 2 tablespoons olive oil for cooking

Preheat oven to 400°F. Drizzle olive oil on a baking sheet. Cut cherry tomatoes in half and spread on baking sheet. Dash with sea salt and pepper and mix. Bake for 15 to 20 minutes.

In a medium bowl, whisk eggs, garlic, and cheese together. Add egg mixture to a skillet that is lightly coated with olive oil, and cook on low to medium high until done.

Lightly coat another medium skillet with olive oil. Place a tortilla and add egg mixture, roasted tomatoes, sundried tomatoes, and basil, and then place the second tortilla on top. Cook each side for 3 to 5 minutes each. Cut into 4 slices.

Serves 2 to 4

Salad for Breakfast

Salad for breakfast may not sound appetizing at first glance, but this morning treat is as healthy as it is delicious.

Time-saving tip: Cook quinoa and chop ingredients the night before.

1 tablespoon white vinegar
1 egg
½ cup quinoa, cooked
1 cup mixed organic greens
⅓ cup avocado, cubed
4 orange slices
1 tablespoon dried cranberries
1 tablespoon pumpkin seeds
Salt and pepper to taste

Dressing: Drizzle olive oil and balsamic vinegar

In a medium stockpot, fill half way with water and bring to a boil. Next add white vinegar and stir. Crack one egg into the simmering water. You can repeat with more eggs if you are making extra salads. Cook until the egg is white and yolks are runny. Carefully scoop the egg out with a spoon and transfer to a plate.

In a medium pot, cook quinoa according to instructions on the box.

In a medium bowl, add mixed greens. Place cooked quinoa in the middle. Add avocados, oranges, and cranberries, and then place one poached egg on top. Toss pumpkin seeds on the salad.

Drizzle light dressing, and salt and pepper to taste.

Serves 1

Morning Chocolate Surprise

For all the chocolate lovers out there, try this powerhouse breakfast. It is incredibly delicious and may give you a boost to start your day.

Time-saving tip: You can have everything ready the night before.

8 ounces Greek yogurt, plain
½ teaspoon cocoa powder
½ tablespoon honey or pure maple syrup
1 teaspoon chia seeds
1 teaspoon hemp seeds
1 teaspoon organic unsweetened shredded coconut flakes
½ banana, sliced
1 to 2 tablespoons chopped walnuts

In a small bowl, mix yogurt with cocoa powder, honey or pure maple syrup, chia seeds, hemp seeds, and coconut flakes. Add sliced bananas and top with walnuts.

Serves 1

Busy Bee Breakfast Smoothie

This is a great way to start your day with all the necessary vitamins and minerals. It is delicious and simple to prepare.

1 cup vanilla almond milk or filtered water
1 teaspoon organic or raw honey
½ banana
½ apple
1 tablespoon chia seeds
1 scoop protein powder (optional)

Blend all ingredients, and enjoy!

Serves 1

Tacos for Kids

This recipe is great for those picky eaters who don't like anything but plain scrambled eggs.

2 eggs
1 to 2 tablespoons milk of choice (I use unsweetened almond milk)
½ tablespoon olive oil
Shredded cheese (optional)
2 hard taco shells

Directions:

In a small bowl, scramble the eggs with milk (Optional: add cheese in egg mixture).

Lightly coat a small skillet with olive oil and turn on low to medium heat. Next, pour in the egg mixture and cook until fluffy.

Heat oven to 350°F. Place two taco shells on ungreased baking sheet and cook for about 3 minutes.

Fill taco shells with scrambled eggs and serve.

Serves 2

Banana Walnut French Toast

I got the idea of dressing up my French toast from a restaurant I went to many years ago. Before I had seen this menu with different styles of French toast, I would often make mine plain with butter and syrup. This style of French toast is sweet and one of my family's favorite.

Time-saving tip: Make extra and freeze in a tight reclosable plastic bag for another day.

2 eggs
2 tablespoons vanilla almond milk
1/3 teaspoon sea salt
1/2 teaspoon cinnamon
1/4 teaspoon nutmeg
2 tablespoons fresh parsley, chopped
1/2 tablespoon pure maple syrup
2 tablespoons unrefined organic coconut oil, melted
8 slices whole grain bread
1 banana, sliced
1/2 cup of walnuts, toasted

In a medium bowl, add eggs, milk, salt, cinnamon, nutmeg, parsley, and syrup, and mix. Add 1/2 to 1 tablespoon coconut oil to a medium-sized skillet on medium low heat. Next, dunk two slices of bread in egg mixture and place both on skillet. Cook each side until golden brown. Transfer to a plate and cut diagonally. Dress the French toast with banana slices and toasted walnuts. Serve with pure maple syrup.

Makes 8 slices

CHAPTER 11:
Lunch Recipes

Blueberry Burger Salad

I love dining outside in the sun. This is a great lunch for summer-time. If you are cutting back on bread you will love this new twist.

Time-saving tip: You can wash the greens and store them in a bowl.

2 veggie burgers (recipe on page 78)
2 cups mixed greens
½ cup Boston lettuce
1 tablespoon mint leaves, chopped
1 teaspoon shallots, chopped
¼ cup fresh blueberries
2 ounces pecans
2 tablespoons crumbled feta cheese
Dressing:
Juice of one lemon wedge
1 tablespoon extra-virgin olive oil
½ to 1 tablespoon balsamic vinegar
Sea salt and black pepper to taste

Wash mixed greens, Boston lettuce, mint leaves and lay on a paper towel to air dry. Add even amounts of mixed greens, Boston lettuce and mint leaves on two medium-sized plates. Place one burger in the middle of each salad plate. Finally, toss in shallots, blueberries, pecans and feta cheese. For the dressing, whisk together the juice of one lemon wedge, extra-virgin olive oil, balsamic vinegar, sea salt and pepper to taste. Pour desired amount of dressing on salad and serve.

Serves 2

Veggie Burger

You don't have to be vegan to enjoy this version of a meatless burger. You can serve this on a faceless roll, a salad, or with a side of jicama salsa. Another option is to roll them into veggie meatballs for pasta night.

Time-saving tip: Make burgers ahead of time and store in refrigerator, covered. You can also freeze them.

1 15-ounce can of BPA-free black beans, rinsed and drained
1 cup of gluten-free or Italian bread crumbs
1 egg
1 garlic clove, minced
¼ teaspoon sea salt
¼ teaspoon pepper
¼ teaspoon paprika
¼ cup of fresh parsley sprigs, cut up
¼ cup of red onion, finely diced
⅓ cup carrots, shredded
½ cup red bell pepper, finely diced
1 tablespoon ground flaxseed
1 tablespoon of Worcestershire sauce

In a medium bowl, mix all the ingredients and form into six patties. It may be a little sticky.

In a medium skillet, add 1 tablespoon of olive oil and cook each patty for about 2 to 3 minutes on each side.

Yield: 6 patties

Pizza Sandwich

This is a special treat to take to work or on a picnic.

1 to 2 tablespoons of butter
2 slices of gluten-free bread or paleo bread
1 tablespoon marinara sauce
½ cup mozzarella cheese
2 or 3 fresh spinach leaves

Heat a small skillet on medium high and melt ½ tablespoon of butter. Spread sauce on one slice of bread, then cheese and spinach leaves. Butter both sides of the second piece of bread. Put the sandwich together and place in the pan. Heat one side for about 1 minute, and then flip to the other side for another minute. Serve with a side salad.

Serves 1

Vegetable Wrap

Eating healthy tastes so good, especially with this light, crunchy, delightful wrap.

Time-saving tip: You can make extra wraps for lunch the following day, or cut into little pieces and have as an afternoon snack. Also, have your bunch of collard greens washed and shaved for the week. It is best to store them in an air-tight reclosable plastic bag; they should keep fresh for at least a week.

Per wrap:
2 slices yellow bell pepper
1 tablespoon olive oil
1 collard green
1 tablespoon distilled white vinegar (to wash collard green)
3 carrot sticks
2 slices avocado
1 slice red tomato
¼ cup fresh spinach, shredded
1 slice apple, cut in half
½ tablespoon red onion, chopped
2 thin slices cucumber
2 tablespoons plain hummus
Sea salt and pepper to taste

Preheat oven to 400°F. Place slices of yellow bell peppers on a large baking sheet that you've lightly coated with olive oil. Season with sea salt and black pepper. Cook for about 15-30 minute until edges are golden brown, turning once halfway through. Take out of oven and set aside.

While the peppers are roasting, give your collard green a bath in warm vinegar water to clean. Dry the collard green and lay on a flat surface. With a sharp paring knife, carefully shave off the stalk that runs the length of the collard green. It should be the same thickness as the leaf. If you miss this step, the green will not wrap without tearing.

Put one collard green on a cutting board and add all the veggies and apple. Top with 1 to 2 tablespoons of hummus, and roll. Cut in half and serve with a side of brown rice or quinoa.

Serves 1

No-Mayo Egg Salad

This is a great alternative to the traditional egg salad. Be creative and add it to whole grain bread, a wrap, lettuce, or cracker

Time-saving tip: Make extra for the following morning.

4 eggs
1 avocado
½ tablespoon celery seeds
1½ tablespoons shredded fresh parsley
1 tablespoon of olive oil
Sea salt and pepper to taste
1 teaspoon curry powder
1 tablespoon red onion, finely chopped

Boil eggs in a pot of water for about 10 minutes. Peel when cooled. In a medium-sized bowl, mash 2 eggs with yolks and 2 egg whites (discard the yolk). Cut the avocado in half, discard the pit, and add the avocado to the mashed eggs. Add celery seeds, parsley, olive oil, sea salt, pepper, curry powder, red onions, and mix. Refrigerate for a couple hours.

Yield: 1½ cups

Jicama Salsa

I love experimenting and creating colorful dishes in my kitchen. This can be used as a topping for a salad, side dish, or snack for baked pita chips. Another great idea is to add it to a sandwich, wrap, or taco.

Time-saving tip: Make extra to have the following day as a side with dinner or in a wrap for lunch.

½ large jicama, diced or julienned
1 mango, diced
2 tablespoons chopped red onion
1 whole avocado, diced
½ yellow pepper diced
1½ cups of cherry tomatoes, cut in half
¼ cup cilantro, shredded
1 lime, freshly squeezed
¼ cup olive oil
1½ teaspoons ground cumin
Sea salt and pepper to taste

Mix all the ingredients together in a medium-sized bowl and re-frigerate for up to six hours. Serve with tacos, or toss in your salad.

Yield: 3 cups

Vegetarian Fagioli

This is my favorite, especially in the fall. I love to dip a piece of whole grain roll in it.

Time-saving tip: Make extra to freeze for a busy day.

1 16 ounce bag of organic great northern beans
12 cups water
1/3 cup olive oil
3 garlic cloves, minced
2 carrots, washed and sliced
1 whole sweet onion, chopped
1 32-ounce vegetable broth
1 cup crushed tomatoes, organic if possible
2 bay leaves
1 celery stalk
1 teaspoon oregano
1 to 2 teaspoons of Celtic Sea Salt
1 to 2 teaspoons of black pepper
2 tablespoons chopped fresh parsley
1 to 2 cups precooked brown rice, gluten-free pasta, or whole grain pasta

Place northern beans in a large bowl and fill with water. Soak the beans overnight, about 8 hours. Drain and rinse beans the following morning. In a large pot, fill with 8 cups of water and add beans. Bring to a boil: simmer for about 1 1/2 hours, then drain and rinse. Set aside.

Pour olive oil in large stock pot turn to medium heat. Add minced garlic, sliced carrots, and chopped onions, and cook until tender. Add the water and beans and cook until boiling. Reduce heat to medium-low and cook for about an hour.

Add vegetable broth, 1 cup of tomatoes, bay leaves, celery, oregano, salt, pepper, and parsley. Cook on low-medium heat for about 30 to 45 minutes; stir occasionally. Discard bay leaves and celery stalk.

To serve: Add precooked brown rice or pasta to a bowl and serve the hot soup over.

Serves 7 to 12 people

No-Crust Pizza

This is a great way to have pizza without the crust, and it is delicious.

Time-saving tip: Make extra to have the next day in a sandwich or as a side for dinner.

4 medium-large portobello mushroom caps
2 tablespoons extra-virgin olive oil
Sea salt and black pepper to taste
2 garlic cloves, minced
1 medium yellow pepper
2 Roma tomatoes, thinly sliced
1 cup mozzarella cheese
1½ cups fresh arugula

Wash the mushroom caps and dry with a paper towel. Remove the black gills and stems. Preheat the oven to 425°F. Place the mushrooms on a cookie sheet, brush with olive oil, and sprinkle with salt and pepper. Cook for 5 to 7 minutes, remove from oven, and set aside.

Lightly coat a small skillet with ½ tablespoon of extra-virgin olive oil and cook minced garlic and chopped yellow bell pepper until soft. Once cooked, remove and set aside.

Remove mushrooms from the baking sheet to discard water. Place the mushroom caps on a baking sheet lined with wax paper and get ready to build your pizza.

For each mushroom, add 2 to 3 slices of tomato and 1 tablespoon of chopped yellow pepper and garlic mixture. Sprinkle with cheese and top with shredded arugula. Place back in the oven and cook for about 5 minutes until cheese is melted.

Serves 4

Savory Turkey Wimpies in a Bowl

You can create this before you head to bed so it cooks while you sleep. When you wake up in the morning, lunch will be ready for work or school. On a weekend, you can start this process in the morning and cook on high for 3 to 4 hours so it's ready in time for lunch.

Time-saving tip: Make extra to freeze for another day.

2 pounds ground turkey
1 medium sweet onion, finely chopped
1 green pepper, seeded and chopped
3 garlic cloves, minced
2 tablespoons of olive oil
15-ounce of tomato sauce
¾ cup ketchup with *no* high-fructose corn syrup
1 tablespoon Worcestershire sauce
¼ cup unsweetened almond milk
1 teaspoon chili powder

Brown ground turkey in a skillet and drain fat. Put ground turkey to Crockpot; add remaining ingredients while stirring. Cover; turn on low and cook 8 to 10 hours. Serve on a roll.

Serves 8 to 10

Apple and Pecan Salad

I enjoy picnics in the autumn, especially when the leaves start to change and fall. My favorite place to sit is by a tree in a park while the sun is out, when the air smells earthy and leaves are falling. The combination of apples and pecans remind me of this season. Before you head out for work during the week or go on a picnic on the weekend, be sure to pack an Apple and Pecan Salad to go.

Time-saving tip: Make extra for dinner or add to a wrap for lunch the following day.

1 Fuji apple, chopped, with seeds removed and skin left on
4 cups mixed greens
1 cup Boston lettuce
1 celery stalk, sliced
½ cup toasted pecans
½ cup crumbled feta cheese (optional)
Dressing:
½ cup olive oil
2 lemon wedges, juiced
2 tablespoons balsamic vinegar
Sea salt and pepper to taste

Mix the greens and Boston lettuce together. Toss in remaining ingredients and mix.

Place on individual plates. For dressing, mix ingredients in a bowl and drizzle desired amount over salad.

Serves 2 to 4

Cranberry Chicken Salad

This is a great way to use leftover chicken for a great easy grab-and-go lunch or afternoon snack.

Time-saving tip: Make extra to have the following day for lunch.

4 cups cooked chicken, shredded with fork
½ cup dried cranberries
¼ cup of pecans, chopped
¼ cup of celery, finely sliced
2 tablespoons shallots, finely chopped
1/3 cup of eggless mayonnaise (I use Vegenaise)
½ tablespoon of Worcestershire sauce
Salt and pepper to taste

Mix all the ingredients in a medium-sized bowl and refrigerate for an hour. Serve alone or on a cracker, wrap, or salad.

Yield: 5 cups

White Bean Salad with Cherry Tomatoes and Herbs

I love this salad in the summer. It's great as a side dish for a picnic in your backyard or as lunch for work. You can even add it to a whole grain wrap and make it a wrap sandwich. This is a pinch of deliciousness.

Time-saving tip: You can make extra to have as a side for dinner or breakfast the next day with a side of eggs.

1 cup white beans, rinsed
1½ cups cherry tomatoes, cut in half
1 small cucumber, sliced, with or without the skin
1 handful fresh basil, shredded
½ cup fresh cilantro, shredded
2 tablespoons chives, thinly sliced
½ to 1 cup small mozzarella balls
1 garlic clove, minced
4 tablespoons extra-virgin olive oil
2 tablespoons balsamic vinegar
Sea salt and black pepper to taste

Add all the ingredients in a medium-sized bowl to combine. Mix well. Serve at room temperature or refrigerate for 30 minutes before serving.

Serves: 2

Pomegranate Salad

This looks so pretty and festive, especially for Christmas. This is great side dish for lunch. If you have extra pomegranate seeds check out the *Pomegranate Berry Smoothie* recipe in chapter 14.

Time-saving tip: Make extra to have for dinner.

1 cup kale, chopped
1 cup spinach, chopped
1 tablespoon green onions, thinly sliced
½ cup pomegranate seeds
¼ cup raw or toasted pecans
¼ cup feta cheese
Sea salt and pepper to taste
2 tablespoons extra-virgin olive oil
1 tablespoon balsamic vinegar

In a medium-sized bowl, combine all the ingredients and mix. If you are taking it for lunch, put the extra-virgin olive oil and vinegar (or your favorite dressing) in a separate container until ready to serve.

Serves: 2

Roasted Eggplant Berry Sandwich

Did you know that eggplant is a berry? What a great berry sandwich to make on a less busy day by preparing the eggplant and red bell pepper for roasting.

Time-saving tip: Roast extra red peppers and eggplant to have during the week in your eggs, salad, or sandwich.

1 small eggplant berry, cut in half and cut into ¼-inch slices
Sea salt and black pepper to taste
2 to 4 tablespoons of extra-virgin olive oil
Red bell peppers, cut into quarters
4 slices of Ezekiel bread or favorite hard, whole grain roll
1 garlic clove
2 half-dollar sized slices of mozzarella cheese
4 to 8 fresh basil leaves

Preheat oven to 400°F. Sprinkle eggplant slices with sea salt. Place in a strainer over a bowl for about 15 minutes, and then press out the liquid.

Spray a baking sheet with olive oil. Place eggplant slices on the sheet and drizzle with olive oil. Roast for 30 to 40 minutes until slightly brown and tender. Tip: you can do this in advance.

In the meantime, prep your red bell peppers. Wash each pepper and pat dry. Cut into quarters and place on another baking sheet that has been lightly coated with olive oil. Sprinkle each bell pepper with sea salt and pepper. Drizzle with olive oil and massage through. Roast for about 30 minutes. Once they bubble and turn a slight golden brown on the edges, remove from oven and set aside.

After the eggplant is cooked, remove from oven and set aside.

Lightly brush both sides of your Ezekiel bread or favorite hard whole grain roll with olive oil. Cut garlic clove in half and rub against each side of bread or roll. Place 1 or 2 slices of roasted eggplant and two quarter pieces of red bell pepper on one piece of bread and one slice of mozzarella cheese on the other. Place on a baking sheet in the oven, watching closely until the cheese bubbles and the edge of the bread is slightly golden brown.

Remove from oven. Place basil leaves on the piece of bread with cheese on it, and fold the two slices together. Return to oven and toast on each side until golden brown.

Yield: 2 servings

Mexican Potato Tacos

This is a good dish to serve for lunch and you can theme it Mexican Fiesta. It's fun to pick and choose which ingredients to have on top of the potato. Don't forget to wear the sombrero hat and play some music.

4 small sweet potatoes
2 tablespoons organic butter
Sea salt and black pepper to taste
Shredded taco (part-skim) cheese (optional)
1 cup black beans (BPA-free can), drained and rinsed
2 ripe avocados, mashed
1 lemon, squeezed
1 tablespoon olive oil
1 jalapeño pepper, minced
1 garlic clove, minced
1 pound ground turkey
½ tablespoon chili powder
½ tablespoon cumin powder
½ tablespoon garlic powder
4 tablespoons salsa
4 tablespoons Greek yogurt, plain

Directions:

Fill a medium-sized pot halfway with water and bring to a boil. Peel potatoes and cut into cubes. Put the potatoes in the pot of water and boil for 30 minutes or until soft. Drain the water out of the pot, leaving the potatoes behind.

In a glass bowl, add the potatoes and mash with 2 tablespoons of butter, a pinch of sea salt and pepper, and set aside.

Place 1½ cups of mashed sweet potatoes in each of four bowls.

In a separate small bowl, mash avocados with a fork. Mix in freshly squeezed juice of one lemon, and season with a pinch of sea salt and pepper. Set aside.

In a medium skillet, lightly coat pan with olive oil, and add jalapeño pepper and minced garlic. Cook for 2 minutes; then add ground turkey. Season with chili powder, cumin, and garlic powder. Cover and stir until meat is browned. Drain the fat and add turkey to a medium-sized bowl.

Put salsa, cheese, black beans, Greek yogurt and avocado mixture in separate bowls.

Build your taco with the above ingredients.

Serves 4

Apple-Yam Salad

This is a great salad for any time of year, especially in the fall. I like to pair with chicken or pork tenderloin.

Time-saving tip: Make extra to have the following day for breakfast or lunch. You can add it as a side with a sunny-side up egg or lunch sandwich. It's also great to add in a chicken or pork tenderloin wrap.

1 medium organic yam
2 organic apples
2 celery stalks (organic)
¼ organic red cabbage
Handful of raw, organic spinach
Dressing:
2 tablespoons hemp oil
2 tablespoons freshly squeezed lemon juice
2 garlic cloves, minced
½ tablespoon ginger, minced
2 tablespoons toasted sesame seeds

Using the julienne disc of a food processor, shred the yam and apple to make it look like match sticks. Cut the celery into thin slices. To cut the cabbage, place on a cutting board and cut in half right through the stem. Throw the stem away, place the cabbage on the board, and cut into long slices. Shred the spinach with kitchen scissors. Add shredded yams, apples, celery slices, spinach and red cabbage in a medium bowl and mix. For the dressing, mix in hemp oil, freshly squeezed lemon juice, garlic, and ginger. Add toasted sesame seeds. Mix well.

Serves 2 to 4

Avocado with Roasted Bell Pepper and Pineapple Sandwich

This is a really delicious sandwich. Once you prepare everything on your less busy day, it's a pinch to put together.

Time-saving tip: Cut the pineapple and peppers and roast in advance. Make extra for a snack or salad. Also, you can buy roasted peppers in a jar at the market.

8 slices of bread, gluten free or Ezekiel
4 1/3-inch slices of pineapples, cored
1 red bell pepper, cut into quarters
1 avocado, sliced
4 tablespoons hummus
2 tablespoons olive oil
Sea salt and black pepper
1 tablespoon dried dill

Preheat oven to 400°F. Place pineapple and red bell pepper on a large baking sheet that you've lightly coated with olive oil. Season with sea salt, black pepper, and sprinkle dried dill on all four pineapple slices and red bell pepper. Cook for about 30 minute until edges are golden brown, turning once halfway through. Take out of oven and set aside.

Cut the avocado in half, remove the pit, and scoop the avocado out of the two shells. Lay the two avocado halves on a cutting board and cut each into four slices.

Toast your bread and set aside.

For each sandwich, spread one tablespoon of plain hummus on one slice of bread. Add two slices of avocado, one slice of roasted pineapple, and one piece of roasted bell pepper. Place the two slices of bread together and cut in half.

Serves 4

Roasted Vegetable Wrap

This is a delicious wrap to take to work. Refer to Chapter 12 for the roasted vegetable recipe.

2 whole grain wraps
1 cup roasted vegetables (recipe on page 114)
¼ cup black beans, drained and rinsed
2 slices provolone cheese
1 cup arugula leaves
2 to 4 tablespoons plain hummus

On each wrap, spread 1 to 2 tablespoons of plain hummus. Add ½ cup of roasted vegetables, 1½ tablespoons black beans, one slice provolone cheese, and ½ cup arugula. Roll the wraps and cut in half. Serve with a small bowl of cubed roasted pineapples.

Serves 2

Banana Wrap

This makes a delicious and healthy lunch, and your kids may agree. Collard greens are large leaves from the cabbage family. They are a good replacement for a whole grain wrap. Also, collard wraps travel well because they don't get soggy, making this a great lunch for day trips.

Time-saving tip: Wash and shave a bunch of collard greens for the week and store in an airtight reclosable plastic bag; they should keep fresh for at least a week.

½ yellow bell pepper, roasted
½ orange bell pepper, roasted
1 tablespoon of olive oil
1 tablespoon of balsamic vinegar
Salt and pepper, to taste
2 large collard green leaves, washed and dried
1 tablespoon distilled white vinegar, warmed (to wash the collard greens)
2 bananas, peeled
8 sundried tomatoes, oil packed
2 slices avocado
3 tablespoons plain hummus

Preheat oven to 425°F. Cut yellow and orange bell peppers into 4 slices each. Drizzle with olive oil and balsamic vinegar. Add sea salt and pepper to taste, and mix. Cook for 25 minutes or until edges are golden brown. Once done, take out of the oven to cool.

While the peppers are roasting, give your collard greens a bath in warm vinegar water to clean. Dry the collard greens and lay on a flat surface. With a sharp paring knife, carefully shave off the stalk that runs the length of the collard greens. This should be the same thickness as the leaf. If you skip this step, the green will not wrap without tearing.

To each collard green leaf, add a peeled banana, four sundried tomatoes, a slice of avocado, two slices of yellow and orange bell pepper, and 1½ tablespoons of hummus. Tuck in both sides of the collard green and roll; cut diagonally. Serve with a side of pasta.

Serves 2 to 4

CHAPTER 12:
Dinner Menu

Chicken in a Slow Cooker

This is great recipe for a busy day. You can pair it with roasted orange asparagus and brown rice.

3 to 4 pound whole chicken, organic if possible
1 to 2 tablespoons of butter
Sprigs of fresh rosemary
Sprigs of fresh parsley
2 garlic cloves
Sea salt and pepper to taste
1½ cups chicken broth
1 carrot, cut in half
½ small onion, sliced
2 tablespoons olive oil

Wash whole chicken and remove giblets. Rub the outside of the chicken with butter and place the herbs on top, sprinkle with garlic, sea salt, and black pepper. Pour broth in the slow cooker and add your chicken. Add the carrots and onions. Drizzle olive oil, sea salt, and black pepper over the chicken. Cook on low for 6 to 7 hours or on high for 3 to 4.

Serves 4 to 6

Roasted Orange Asparagus

This is a healthy side dish that you can pair with chicken.

Time-saving tip: Wash and cut your asparagus on your less busy day. If you have extra leftover from dinner, you can add it to your scrambled eggs the following morning.

2 pounds asparagus—wash, cut ½-inch off from the bottom, and cut in thirds
2 garlic cloves, minced
½ tablespoon fresh grated ginger
2 tablespoons olive oil
1 cup sliced baby portobello mushrooms
Pinch of sea salt
¼ teaspoon black pepper
2 to 3 tablespoons freshly squeezed juice of an orange

Preheat oven to 450°F. In a medium-sized bowl add asparagus, garlic, ginger, 1 tablespoon of olive oil, mushrooms, salt and pepper. Mix well.

Lightly coat a baking sheet with 1 tablespoon of olive oil and layer with vegetables. Roast for 10 to 15 minutes. Using an oven mitt, carefully remove baking sheet from oven to mix the vegetables using kitchen prongs. Return to oven for another 10 minutes until the vegetables are a golden brown.

Put on a serving plate, and drizzle with orange juice.

Health Hearty Minestrone Soup

I got this delicious recipe from my mother-in-law. She often served the family this soup on a cold night.

Time-saving tip: Make batches and freeze for busy days.

2 small potatoes, peeled and quartered
¼ cup olive oil
1 yellow onion, finely diced
3 celery stalks, diced and keeping the leaves
2 medium carrots, sliced
½ cup water
1 teaspoon dry parsley
1 garlic clove, minced
16-ounce jar of crushed tomatoes
1 48-ounce chicken broth
1 15-ounce frozen bag of kidney beans
¼ cup frozen green beans
¼ cup frozen lima beans
¼ cup of frozen corn
1 cup frozen peas
1 bag spinach, cut up
1 cup brown rice, cooked

In a medium-sized pot, boil 2 small quartered potatoes until soft. Remove from stove and mash. Set aside.

Add oil and onion to a large pot, and sauté until transparent. Add celery, carrots, parsley, garlic and ½ cup water to pot and cook for 2 minutes. Add crushed tomatoes and cook for 5 minutes. Next, add chicken broth, kidney beans, green beans, lima beans, corn and peas, and simmer for an hour. Toss in mashed potatoes and spinach. Cover for a few more minutes until spinach is soft. Serve with ½ cup of brown rice in each bowl.

Serves: 6 to 8

Friday Night Potato Pizza

It's Friday night, so let's get this pizza party started.

2 medium-sized potatoes
8 tablespoons organic pizza sauce
8 tablespoons mozzarella cheese
Olive oil
Suggested toppings:
Mushrooms
Sweet peppers
Olives
Fresh herbs

Preheat oven to 400°F. Scrub potatoes and pat dry. Poke a couple of holes into each potato using a fork. Set on a baking sheet and bake for about an hour. Remove from oven using an oven mitt, and set aside.

Cut each potato in half. Scoop 2 to 3 tablespoons out of each potato and put in a bowl. (You can use this for mashed potatoes the next day for dinner.) Lightly coat a baking sheet with olive oil and place potato skins side down on the sheet. Begin building your pizza. Start with 1 to 2 tablespoons of pizza sauce, 1 to 2 tablespoons of shredded cheese, and then add your favorite vegetables and herbs. Preheat oven to 350°F and bake your potato pizza until cheese bubbles.

Serves 2 to 4

Roasted Vegetables

These vegetable are scrumptious served right out of the oven, at room temperature, or cold. You can serve them as a side with meat, over a salad, in a wrap, or in rice. Another option is to turn leftovers into another meal the next day by adding quinoa, roasted pine nuts, and feta cheese.

Time-saving tip: Make a big batch on a less busy day.

1 red pepper, cut in strips
1 orange pepper, cut in strips
1 yellow pepper, cut into strips
1 medium zucchini, halved and diced into ½-inch cubes
1 yellow squash, halved and diced into ½-inch cubes
1 cup portobello mushrooms
½ medium red onion, sliced
Half a medium eggplant, diced into ½-inch cubes
1 to 2 tablespoons extra-virgin olive oil
1 to 2 tablespoons balsamic vinegar
2 garlic cloves, minced
1 teaspoon dried basil
Sea salt and pepper, to taste

Preheat oven to 425°F. Spread the vegetables evenly on a baking sheet. Drizzle with extra-virgin olive oil and vinegar. Sprinkle with garlic, dried basil, salt and pepper to taste. Massage through with your hands. Place on the top rack of the oven for 30 to 40 minutes. Stir a couple times and take out of the oven when the edges are slightly brown.

Serves 4

Veggie Zucchini Boats

It's summer, and you have an overabundance of zucchinis. I came up with this delicious recipe a few years ago, and it has been one of my family's favorite dinners. You can serve this with a side salad or grilled chicken.

Time-saving tip: Prepare these ahead of time and store in a covered glass pan in the refrigerator for up to two days.

3 medium zucchinis, washed and cut in half lengthwise
Sea salt and pepper to taste
1 cup brown rice or quinoa, cooked
2 tablespoons of olive oil
1 small sweet onion, finely diced
1 small yellow bell pepper, finely diced
1 cup mushrooms, washed and chopped
½ cup of oil-packed sundried tomatoes, thinly sliced (discard oil)
1 tablespoon of fresh parsley, chopped
3 tablespoons roasted pine nuts
1 cup of shredded, part-skim mozzarella cheese (optional)

Preheat oven to 375°F. Wash and dry zucchinis. Cut both ends off and cut in half lengthwise. Scoop the middle out of both sides of the zucchinis. Place each zucchini half, skin side down on a baking sheet that has been lightly coated with olive oil. Add a pinch of sea salt and black pepper to each zucchini. Place in the oven and cook for 30 to 45 minutes until zucchini is soft.

While the zucchinis are in the oven, cook the rice or quinoa according to the instructions on the box. In a medium skillet, add 1 tablespoon of olive oil and sauté onions, peppers, and mushrooms until softened, about 7 to 10 minutes. Remove and set aside. In a medium bowl, combine cooked rice or quinoa, onions, peppers, mushrooms, sundried tomatoes, and parsley, and mix.

Once zucchinis are cooked, remove from the oven and scoop even amounts of the veggie and quinoa or rice mixture onto each zucchini half. Place back in the oven for another 10 minutes. Put pine nuts on another small baking sheet, and drizzle with olive oil. Place in the oven and roast for a minute or so. Watch closely.

Once zucchini with mixture is cooked, take out of the oven. Toss ½ tablespoon of pine nuts and add 1 to 2 tablespoons of mozzarella cheese on top of each zucchini. Place back into oven and bake until cheese is bubbly and edges are slightly golden brown. Remove and serve.

Serves 3 to 6

Basil Pesto Chicken

You can pair this with a side of vegetables, quinoa, or rice.

Time-saving tip: Make extra to add to your salad or sandwich the following day.

½ cup extra-virgin olive oil
½ cup fresh parsley sprigs
1 cup fresh basil leaves
¼ cup pine nuts
1 medium garlic clove
¼ teaspoon lemon zest
1/3 teaspoon sea salt
¼ teaspoon black pepper
4 boneless, skinless chicken breasts

In a food processor, combine extra-virgin olive oil, parsley, basil, pine nuts, garlic, salt, lemon zest and pepper; blend until a creamy consistency. You may need a little more extra-virgin olive oil if the pesto is too thick.

Rinse chicken breasts and pat dry. Add all four chicken breasts and pesto to a reclosable plastic bag. Shake the bag back and forth to get pesto on all four chicken breasts. Refrigerate for an hour.

Cook chicken: you can grill, sauté, cook in a slow cooker on low for 8 hours, or bake in the oven at 375°F until internal temperature reaches 170°F or until juices run clear when you cut into the chicken.

Serves 4

Tomato-Basil Salad

This is a great summer salad that you can pair with Basil-Pesto Chicken, or put on top of brown rice.

2 cups cherry tomatoes, halved
2 small cucumbers, sliced, with or without skin
1/3 cup red onion, finely chopped
1/4 cup olive oil
1/3 cup extra balsamic vinegar
Sea salt and pepper, to taste
1 tablespoon oregano
1 cup fresh basil, shredded
1/2 cup crumbled feta cheese (optional)

In a medium-sized bowl, combine all the ingredients and mix. Refrigerate for 45 minutes before serving.

Serves 2 to 4

Raw Rainbow Salad

This is terrific in the spring or summer for a picnic or barbeque. You can pair this with chicken or wasabi halibut.

¼ red cabbage, washed and shredded
1 green bell pepper, washed and finely diced
1 green squash, washed and julienned using a food processor
2 carrots, washed and julienned using a food processor
1½ cups cherry tomatoes, washed and halved
1 cup lima beans, cooked and cooled
1 garlic clove, minced
2 tablespoons red onion, finely diced
2 tablespoons hemp seeds
Dressing:
2 tablespoons tahini
1 small garlic clove, minced
1 teaspoon of ginger, minced
¼ cup olive oil
1 tablespoon water
1 teaspoon of raw coconut aminos (soy-free seasoning sauce)
1 juice of an orange
Sea salt and pepper to taste

In a medium bowl, combine all the vegetables. Mix and set aside. In a separate small bowl, combine all of the dressing ingredients, and mix. (Makes ½ cup.)

Add the dressing and hemp seeds to the vegetables, and mix. You may add a little more olive oil. Another option for dressing is: ¼ cup olive oil and balsamic vinegar.

Marinade in refrigerator for 45 minutes before serving.

Serves 2 to 4

Honey Balsamic Pulled Pork

This makes a perfect pairing with Rainbow Salad. Serve alone or on a roll.

Time-saving tip: Make extra to have the following day for lunch.

¼ cup balsamic vinegar
¼ organic honey
¼ cup olive oil
½ cup sweet onion
1 tablespoon fresh rosemary
2 garlic cloves, minced
1 teaspoon fresh ginger, shredded
Dash of sea salt and black pepper
1 to 2 pound pork tenderloin

In a medium-sized bowl, combine all the ingredients except for the pork tenderloin, and mix. Add the pork tenderloin and mixture to a reclosable plastic freezer bag; leave in the refrigerator for about 2 hours to marinade.

Add ½ cup of water to a Crockpot, and then the pork and marinade. Cook on low for 8 to 9 hours.

Take pork out of the Crockpot. Shred pork, using a fork. You can serve with a roll or put on top of brown rice.

Serves 4 to 6

Salmon with Tomatoes and Veggies

This is an all-in-one pan dinner.

A bunch asparagus, cut in half
1 yellow squash, cut into slices
1 lemon
2 tablespoons olive oil
4 salmon filets, wild-caught if possible
1 pint cherry tomatoes
1 garlic clove, minced

Preheat oven to 400°F.

Place asparagus and squash in a large glass pan, and squeeze half a lemon and a little olive oil on top of veggies. Add the salmon fillets, skin side down. Add the tomatoes and toss in garlic. Drizzle olive oil and squeeze the other half of the lemon over the tomatoes and salmon.

Place in the oven and cook for 20 to 30 minutes. Salmon should be pink and flake when you stick a fork in it.

Serves 4

Berry Shrimp Salad

Salads are full of goodness, and that's why this makes a perfect dinner.

Time-saving tip: Make extra to have during the week for lunches. You can add it to a wrap, or have it as a main course.

3 cups mixed greens
3 cups watercress
12 jumbo shrimp, precooked and shells removed
½ cup cilantro, chopped
½ red onion, diced
½ cup blueberries
½ cup raspberries
1 cup quinoa, cooked
¼ cup goat cheese, crumbled
¼ cup toasted pecans, chopped
Dressing: ¼ cup sherry balsamic vinegar, ½ cup olive oil, sea salt and pepper to taste. Mix together in a bowl.
Optional: Pair with salmon or grilled chicken.

In a large bowl, combine all the ingredients, except dressing and mix. Keep in refrigerator until ready to serve. Follow instructions on cooked frozen shrimp bag for defrosting.

Serves: 2 to 4

Scallops Marinara with Whole Grain Penne Pasta

This is one of my favorite recipes, especially in the spring. I hope you enjoy it as much as I do.

2 tablespoons olive oil
A pinch of red pepper flakes
2 tablespoons red onion, finely chopped
2 garlic cloves, minced
12-24 ounces bay scallops (wild caught)
1 15-ounce diced tomatoes
2 tablespoons parsley, chopped
3 tablespoons fresh basil, shredded
¼ cup capers, drained
¼ teaspoon black pepper and sea salt
1 pound whole grain penne pasta

In a medium skillet, heat olive oil on medium. Add a pinch of red pepper flakes, onions and garlic; cook for about 3 minutes or until opaque. Add scallops to pan and cook 2 to 3 minutes or until they are a pale-golden color. Remove scallops and set aside.

Add tomatoes, parsley, basil and capers to pan. Keep stirring until thickened, about 5 minutes. Add the scallops and cook for another 1 to 2 minutes. Season with salt and pepper.

In a medium stockpot, boil water and cook penne pasta until al dente. Drain the pasta in strainer. Next, add to the pan with the scallop marinara. Toss everything together.

Serves 4

Lazy Stuffed Pepper Soup

If you're looking for a soup that is delicious and healthy, check out this one that my sister-in-law, Heather, shared with me. This is made in a Crockpot, which is perfect for those busy days. It's especially nice to come home to find supper already done. You can serve this with toasted flat bread or your favorite roll.

Time-saving tip: Make extra to freeze for busy days.

1 cup onion, chopped
2 green peppers, chopped
1 pound ground turkey
½ teaspoon black pepper
1 cup tomato sauce
1 quart tomatoes, pureed in blender
2 tablespoons margarine
2-½ tablespoons whole wheat or gluten-free flour
1 cup milk (I used unsweetened almond milk)
2 cups brown rice

Add onions, green peppers, ground turkey, black pepper, tomato sauce, and tomatoes to Crockpot. Cook on low for eight hours.

Prior to serving, add margarine, flour, and milk to the soup. Stir well.

Follow package directions to cook brown rice.

Spoon desired amount of rice into soup bowl, then add soup. Optional: Top with shredded cheese.

Serves 6

Wasabi Halibut

This is a tangy and savory dish that you can serve with rice and Rainbow Salad. This is a nice dish to have for two.

Time-saving tip: Make extra for fish tacos or in a salad the following day.

4 halibut fillets
2 tablespoons raw coconut aminos (soy-free seasoning sauce)
2 teaspoons sesame oil
1 tablespoon fresh lime juice
1 teaspoon wasabi paste
1 teaspoon ginger, freshly grated
1 garlic clove, minced
2 tablespoons sesame seeds

Preheat oven to 425°F. In a bowl, add the raw coconut aminos, sesame oil, lime juice, wasabi past, ginger and garlic, and mix. Lay the halibut in a single layer in a glass pan. Pour mixture over top, and place in oven for about 10 minutes. Sprinkle sesame seeds on top of each fillet, and place back in the oven for 5 to 10 more minutes. Remove from oven.

Serves 4

Cherry Chicken Skewers

This is perfect for the summer, especially when cherries are in season. You can buy a bag of frozen cherries, or pit fresh cherries and freeze them in a reclosable plastic bag. You can pair this with a salad.

Time-saving tip: Make extra for the following day for lunch or dinner in a wrap, salad, or pasta.

1 teaspoon olive oil
2 tablespoons raw coconut aminos (soy-free seasoning sauce)
1 tablespoon balsamic vinegar
1 garlic clove, minced
½ teaspoon ginger, minced
½ teaspoon organic sugar
2 tablespoons sweet onion, finely chopped
½ cup of cherries, pitted and chopped
Black pepper to taste
1½ pounds chicken breast, rinsed and cubed

In a food processor, add oil, raw coconut aminos, vinegar, garlic, ginger, sugar, onions, cherries and black pepper. Blend until smooth to create a marinade. In a bowl or large reclosable plastic bag, add chicken cubes and marinade (keep some marinade reserved for basting) and refrigerate for 2 to 4 hours. Once the chicken has finished marinating, add chicken to 3 or 4 skewers.

Preheat oven to 450°F degrees. Lightly coat a baking sheet with olive oil and add chicken skewers. Bake about 15 minutes then brush with reserved marinade and turn once. Bake for another 20 to 25 minutes. To check for doneness, cut one chicken cube in half to make sure the chicken is cooked thoroughly through.

Serves 4

Pasta Squash with Pesto Sauce

Zucchini is a healthy alternative to pasta. I love this version, especially in the summer when I don't want to cook using the stove. I usually have this with a side salad and cold glass of water.

1 medium zucchini, julienned
1 small yellow squash, julienned
1 cup fresh basil
½ cup fresh parsley sprigs
2 small garlic cloves
½ to 1 cup olive oil
1 teaspoon lemon zest
¼ cup walnuts
Sea salt and pepper to taste
Basil leaves, for presentation (optional)
Walnuts, for presentation (optional)
Parmesan cheese (optional)

Cut the squash in your food processor with the julienne disc. If you have a spiralizer, great. You can spiralize both squash in a bowl.

Set your julienned (or spiralized) squash aside. In a food processor, blend basil, parsley, garlic, olive oil, lemon zest, walnuts, and salt and pepper to taste. Add the pesto sauce on top of the bowl of squash. Top with two basil leaves and a few walnuts for presentation. Serve at room temperature. Optional: sprinkle with parmesan cheese.

Serves 4

Roasted Cauliflower with Garden Vegetables and Capers

This can be a main dish or side dish. Pair with grilled fish or chicken.

2 tablespoons of hemp oil
2 medium-sized garlic cloves, minced
¼ teaspoon red pepper flakes
1 full organic cauliflower, washed and cut into slices, keeping some of the leaves
Sea salt and black pepper to taste
1 cup organic cherry tomatoes, washed and cut in half
1 yellow bell pepper, washed and diced
2 tablespoons organic capers, rinsed and drained
1 tablespoon fresh parsley, chopped
Optional: Roasted sliced almonds and/or parmesan cheese

In a medium-sized skillet, heat hemp oil on medium heat. Add garlic and red pepper flakes. Add cauliflower and season with sea salt and pepper to taste. Cook about 25 minutes, turning the cauliflower several times. After it turns a little brown, add the tomatoes, yellow peppers, capers, parsley and cauliflower leaves, and cook for a couple more minutes. Optional: add almonds and parmesan cheese.

Serves 2 to 4

CHAPTER 13:
Delicious Dessert

Summertime Fruit Berry Dessert

This is a refreshing dessert to serve your family poolside or on a picnic. Optional: You can eat it as is, or add it to plain yogurt or sherbet.

1 to 2 cups blackberries
1 to 2 cups sliced strawberries
1 to 2 cups blueberries
1 to 2 cups raspberries
2 peaches, sliced, pit removed
2 plums, sliced
2 kiwis, skin removed and sliced
Juice from 2 freshly squeezed oranges
1/3 cup of organic sugar
1/2 tablespoon of fresh mint leaves, shredded

Toss the sliced fruit in a bowl. Squeeze in juice of 2 oranges, sprinkle sugar and mix. Toss in mint leaves and mix. Refrigerate 4 to 6 hours and then serve.

Serves 2 to 4

Berry-licious Ice Pops

When I was growing up, summertime meant playing outside from sunup to sundown. Although I was involved in a lot of active sports and playtime, there was nothing like hearing the other kids in the neighborhood shouting, "The ice cream truck is here!" I remember running into the house to beg my mother for fifty cents to buy a refreshing soft chocolate ice cream cone—my favorite. Nowadays, I enjoy making my own for my family to enjoy. Not only will your kids love this frozen treat, so will you.

1 cup organic strawberries blended with ¼ cup of water or almond milk
1 cup pineapple blended with ¼ cup water or almond milk
1 cup of organic blueberries blended with ¼ cup of water or almond milk

Note: you can use any fruit for this recipe.

Fill about 1 to 2 tablespoons of each fruit into the mold (I use Zoku Quick Pop Maker).

Freeze for about 10 minutes.

After they are frozen, pop out and enjoy!

If you don't have a Popsicle maker, you can fill paper cups with each blended fruit and insert a Popsicle stick. (This process will take a little longer—a few hours.)

Enjoy these cool, healthy, and sweet treats.

Serves 6

Chocolate Banana Delight

This is a refreshing and delightful homemade ice cream. You'll need a high-speed blender to make this sweet dessert.

4 frozen bananas, cut in half
2 teaspoons of cacao powder
1 teaspoon unsweetened almond milk
¼ cup of blackberries, smashed
1 tablespoon chopped walnuts

Freeze your bananas in a reclosable plastic bag or container. In a high speed blender, add your bananas, almond milk and cacao powder, and blend on high until creamy. In a small bowl, smash blackberries with the back of a fork. Scoop half the banana mixture into two small bowls. Add about 1 tablespoon of smashed blackberries on top of each scoop of banana ice cream. Top each with ½ tablespoon of nuts.

Serves 2

Sweet Chocolate Date

There is nothing like the comfort of a sweet date while the kids are in school. Not only is this date delicious, but healthy too! You can make extra and store in the freezer. They're great when you're in the mood for something sweet.

10 dates, pitted
½ teaspoon pure maple syrup
2 tablespoons filtered water
¼ cup goji berries
1 cup unsweetened shredded coconut flakes; reserve ½ cup to roll balls in
2 tablespoons raw chocolate cacao powder
2 tablespoons hemp seeds
1 tablespoon coconut oil, melted
Pinch of Celtic Sea Salt
2 tablespoons cacao nibs (optional)

In a food processor, blend all the ingredients until smooth. If needed, add a little more water. The mixture should be sticky. Roll 12 balls in reserved coconut flakes. Place in a glass dish and refrigerate for about an hour.

Serves: 6 to 12

Berry Summer Pie

1 cup blueberries
½ cup blackberries
1½ cups raspberries
4 kiwis, peeled and sliced
2 cups strawberries, washed and sliced
4 whole strawberries, washed
½ cup pineapple, sliced
¼ cup organic sugar
Organic whip cream
For crust:
½ cup almonds
2 tablespoons hemp seeds
1½ cups pecans
½ tablespoon cinnamon
12 fresh dates, pitted
2 tablespoons unrefined organic coconut oil, melted

In a food processor, combine almonds, hemp seeds, pecans, cinnamon and mix. Next, add pitted dates, coconut oil and blend until it forms into a ball. Remove crust mixture from food processor and transfer to an 8-inch glass pie dish and spread crust in; pat firmly down and on the sides. Place in the freezer for 30 minutes. Take out and refrigerate for about 2 hours.

Mix each fruit in a separate bowl with 1 to 2 teaspoons of sugar. Set aside. After 2 hours, take crust out of the refrigerator. Place sliced strawberries on the bottom, covering the whole pie. Layer with sliced kiwi, and then a few blueberries. Arrange raspberries around the inside edge of the circle. Place pineapples in the middle of pie with blackberries and blueberries. Add whole strawberries around the pie; finish with whip cream (optional). See picture for presentation.

Serves 8

Honey Roasted Pear and Yogurt

1 tablespoon unrefined organic coconut oil
2 pears, stems and seeds removed, halved
3 tablespoons honey
3 cups Greek yogurt, plain
½ teaspoon vanilla extract
1 tablespoon pure maple syrup
½ cup pecans and granola, mixed
1 teaspoon cinnamon

Preheat the oven 425°F. Spread coconut oil in a medium-sized baking sheet. Place pears cut side up on baking sheet and drizzle with honey. Roast for about 40 minutes. Once done, take out of the oven and allow to cool. In a medium bowl, mix yogurt with vanilla extract and maple syrup.

Evenly divide yogurt into four small bowls. Place a roasted pear in each bowl, and add even amounts of nuts and granola between the bowls. Optional: sprinkle with cinnamon.

Serves 4

Watermelon Slushie

This is a refreshing summer dessert.

4 cups seedless watermelon, cubed
¼ cup fresh squeezed lemon juice
1 tablespoon organic sugar
1 tablespoon fresh mint leaves
2 cups ice

Directions:

In a blender, blend all ingredients.

Serves 2-4

Raspberry Tea Jell-O Gelatin

This is a delicious dessert for anytime of the year.

4 organic raspberry teabags
3 cups boiled water
1 cup cold water
1 box plain gelatin
2 tablespoons organic honey
1 cup raspberries
Organic whip cream (optional)

Boil 3 cups of water. Steep three raspberry teabags in boiling water for about 5 minutes and one raspberry teabag in a cup of cold water. In a large bowl, add one cup of cold raspberry tea and sprinkle packets of gelatin; let stand for 1 minute. Add hot raspberry tea and stir until gelatin dissolves. Add 2 tablespoons of honey and stir. Pour gelatin mixture into a 9x13 glass pan, and evenly add raspberries. Refrigerate for 3 to 4 hours. Once firm, cut into squares, and serve with a dollop of organic whip cream if desired.

Serves 12 to 18

CHAPTER 14:
Healthy Smoothies

have been on a smoothie kick since my transformation. I love sailing through the fruit and veggie aisles or exploring the farmers' market to see what I can get my hands on. Smoothies are great because you get a lot of nutritional benefit from simply blending fruits and vegetables. It's one of my family's favorite meal or snack replacement for busy days.

Gingerbread Man Smoothie

1 cup almond or organic milk
1 frozen banana
Handful organic spinach
1 tablespoon organic peanut butter
1 tablespoon unsweetened shredded coconut
½ teaspoon cinnamon
¼ teaspoon ginger
1 teaspoon maple syrup
1 tablespoon molasses
1 tablespoon chia seeds
1 to 2 cups of ice

Blend all ingredients until smooth.

Serves 1 to 2

Ever-Green Smoothie

1 cup organic kale
1 cup organic mixed green lettuce
1 celery stalk
1 kiwi
1 teaspoon flax seeds
2 teaspoons organic honey
1 cup filtered water
1 cup ice

In a high speed blender, blend all ingredients until smooth. If you don't have a high speed blender, blend the greens with water first until smooth and add the other ingredients.

Serves 1 to 2

Pomegranate Berry Smoothie

1 cup almond milk or grass-fed milk
¼ cup frozen blueberries
¼ cup blackberries
¼ cup pomegranate seeds
1 teaspoon chia seeds
½ banana

Blend all ingredients together until smooth.

Serves 1 to 2

Post Workout Smoothie

1 cup filtered water
1 cup ice
½ cup frozen cherries
1 banana
1 scoop protein powder
1 tablespoon cacao nibs
1 tablespoon peanut butter (organic)

Blend all the ingredients together until smooth.
Visit www.SheilaFitnessNHealthyLifestyle.com for my favorite
protein powder.

Serves 1 to 2

Chia Latte Smoothie

This smoothie will make you want to dance in the snow. If you use a high speed blender, you can blend on high speed for a few minutes to warm it up, or you can serve it cold. For the finishing touch, sprinkle some extra cinnamon on top and serve with a cinnamon stick.

1 cup almond or grass-fed milk
1 cup chai latte
1 teaspoon pure maple syrup
Cinnamon
1 tablespoon almond butter
1 teaspoon chia seeds

Blend all ingredients together until smooth.

Serves 1 to 2

Sweet Cherry Smoothie

1 cup almond milk
1 frozen banana
½ cup frozen dark cherries
2 strawberries
1 date
½ cup ice

Blend everything together until smooth.

Serves 1 to 2

Carrot Cupcake Smoothie

If you love carrot cake, you will enjoy this treat.

1 cup vanilla almond milk
1 carrot, halved, cleaned, and bottoms cut off
¼ teaspoon ginger
1 tablespoon walnuts
½ teaspoon cinnamon
½ tablespoon pure maple syrup
1 banana, frozen
1 date, pitted

Blend everything together until smooth.

Serves 1 to 2

Chocolate Joy

1 cup almond milk
1 frozen banana
2 tablespoons cacao powder
½ cup spinach
1 tablespoon pure maple syrup
1 tablespoon cacao nibs
1 tablespoon sunflower butter

Blend everything in a blender until smooth.

Serves 1

Coconut Kiss

½ cup vanilla almond milk
½ cup coconut water
2 tablespoons unsweetened coconut flakes
1 tablespoon honey
1 frozen banana
½ cup Greek yogurt, plain

Blend together in a blender until smooth.

Serves 1

Green Lean Smoothie

1 cup cold, filtered water
½ cup raw spinach, washed and rinsed
½ cup kale, washed and rinsed
1 date
½ cup frozen strawberries
1 tablespoon flax seeds (optional)
½ cup ice

Blend everything together until smooth.

Serves 1 to 2

Berry Bliss

¾ cup almond milk
½ cup Greek yogurt, plain
1 cup fresh strawberries
4 maraschino cherries
¼ cup ice

Blend all ingredients together in a high speed blender until smooth.

Serves 1 to 2

CHAPTER 15:
Healthy Drink Recipes

Green Tea Mocktini

Green tea has many health benefits. In a mocktail, it is a great way to invite some antioxidants to your party.

1 cup green tea (brewed or chilled)
1 whole lime
1 tablespoon pure maple syrup
Ice

Combine 1 cup of green tea and ice in a shaker. Add juice of a whole lime and pure maple syrup. Stir until blended. Strain into a martini glass. Garnish with a slice of lime.

Serves 1

Apple Mocktini

My mother use to say, "An apple a day will keep the doctor away." Apples are a great source of antioxidants, vitamins, minerals, and fiber. Best of all, they are fat free. If you want a little "zing" in your drink, add ¼ teaspoon ginger per 1 apple. Add more if you want extra "zing." Ginger is a powerful anti-inflammatory herb that is good for healthy digestion.

1 whole red organic apple
Pinch of organic sugar
¼ teaspoon fresh ginger

In a juicer, juice one apple into a cup. Juice the ginger in a separate cup. Combine the two ingredients together, add a pinch of sugar, and stir. Pour into a martini glass and serve.

Serves 1

Piña Colada

This is a wonderful poolside drink or for an evening in with your friends. It's a great kiddie cocktail. Coconut water is the next sports drinks and contains electrolytes to replenish your body.

2 overripe bananas
1 cup pineapple, diced
1 cup coconut water
½ cup coconut milk

Blend all ingredients in a blender and serve in a cup. Garnish with a piece of pineapple.

Serves 4

Honeydew-Mint Nojitos

This is a refreshing drink for brunch.

½ cup mint leaves
½ cup freshly squeezed lime juice (about 4 limes)
2 teaspoons organic sugar
One honeydew melon
2 cups ice
Carbonated water

In a medium-sized bowl, combine mint leaves, lime juice and sugar. Using a muddler or wooden spoon, gently muddle the ingredients together to release the delicious flavor and aroma (about 10 seconds), and then set aside. Put one quarter of the melon cubes in a blender at a time, and process until smooth. Using a muddler or back of a wooden spoon, press through a strainer, leaving the pulp behind. Combine the melon juice with lime juice in a large pitcher. Fill 4 to 8 cups with ice. Add the melon and lime juice, and top with carbonated water or soda. You can garnish with a mint leaf.

Servings 4 to 8

Emerald-Green Juice

This is my favorite juice because it is so refreshing and light.

1 lemon
1 cucumber
1 red or green apple
2 celery stalks
2 kale leaves
1 inch fresh ginger

Peel the lemon, peel the cucumber, cut and core the apple, and place in a juicer. Add the celery, kale, and ginger. If you don't have a juicer, you can blend the ingredients in a blender. Use a fine-mesh strainer to strain the juice into a bowl, leaving the pulp behind. Pour the juice in a glass and serve with ice.

Serves 2 to 4

Mint and Raspberry Water

This is a refreshing drink that will also quench your thirst.

32-ounce mason jar or glass pitcher
28 ounces filtered water
½ to 1 cup ice
4 to 5 fresh mint leaves
¼ cup fresh raspberries

Fill a glass pitcher or jar with filtered water, leaving room for ice. Next add mint leaves and raspberries, and let infuse for 45 minutes in the refrigerator before serving.

Serves 2 to 4

Lemon Ginger Water

Want to give your water a little zing? Try this. It's a great alternative to plain lemon water.

48-ounce glass pitcher
46-ounces of water
1 lemon, sliced
1 teaspoon ginger, freshly grated
4 to 6 ounces of club soda
1 cup ice

Fill the glass pitcher or jar with filtered water, leaving room for ice. Next add lemon slices and ginger; mix well. Let the water infuse for about 45 minutes in the refrigerator. Fill an 8-ounce glass with a couple of ice cubes and 6 ounces of infused lemon ginger water, and top with an ounce of club soda.

Serves 4 to 6

ABOUT THE AUTHOR

 Sheila Royce Garcia is an author, personal trainer, holistic health coach, and loving mother. She wears many hats and has proven that moms can have and do it all while still providing their families with healthy, home-cooked meals. As a child, Sheila often would be found in the kitchen, whipping up delicious meals for her family to try and enjoy. It all began by learning how to make a peanut butter and jelly sandwich which evolved into cooking pancakes and French toast for breakfast. She has a passion for cooking and is incredibly talented despite never receiving any formal culinary training. She represents all the busy families who try to juggle it all while short on time. She used her vast culinary knowledge and expertise to turn her healthy recipes and tips for cooking on busy days into a cookbook for busy families.

In addition to creating delicious recipes, Sheila has a love for staying fit and eating foods that support her healthy lifestyle. Being active started at a young age for her. She was fortunate enough to have two parents who showed her the benefits of living an active lifestyle. In addition, Sheila was somewhat adventurous with creating home-cooked meals. You would often find her designing dinner themes with her parents as a child, such as veggie night or no-meat night. Her family rarely went out to eat for dinner. When they did eat out, it was a real family treat!

Her business was created to guide women and their families to live a healthy lifestyle by supporting them with weight issues, stress management, creating work and life balance, and eating healthy on busy days. She knows firsthand what it's like to be a mom balancing a family and career, which is why she wants to show other women that being healthy and serving their families nourishing meals is achievable, no matter how busy their schedule may be. Sheila is excited to share this book with her readers, the busy moms and dads whom she had in mind when she crafted it.

www.SheilaRoyceGarcia.com
www.HealthyCookinginaPinch.com
www.facebook.com/sheilafitnessnhealthylifestyle
www.pinterest.com/sheilafitness

INDEX

REFERENCES:

http://www.ewg.org/foodnews/list.php, calendar year 2014
http://www.ewg.org/research, calendar year 2014
http://www.localharvest.org/csa/, calendar year 2014
Lazaroff, C. (2002) http://www.organicconsumers.org/corp/
foodtravel112202.cfm